# ZBIG

## THE MAN WHO CRACKED THE KREMLIN

# ZBIG

## THE MAN WHO CRACKED THE KREMLIN

**ANDRZEJ LUBOWSKI**
*PREFACE BY SHLOMO AVINERI*

All rights reserved, including without limitation the right to reproduce this book or any portion thereof in any form or by any means, whether electronic or mechanical, now known or hereinafter invented, without the express written permission of the publisher.

Copyright © 2011 by Andrzej Lubowski

Translated from Polish by William Brand

Cover design by Maciej Kalkus, drawing by Piotr Lesniak

The author thanks Agora SA for the permission to use the cover from the Polish edition of the book.

ISBN 978-1-4804-6130-7

Distributed in 2013 by Open Road Distribution
345 Hudson Street
New York, NY 10014
www.openroadmedia.com

# TABLE OF CONTENTS

| | |
|---|---:|
| Preface by Shlomo Avineri | *vii* |
| Prologue | *3* |
| Free of Illusions | *11* |
| From Kennedy to Rockefeller | *23* |
| Pygmalion Redux | *35* |
| A Piano Piece for Four Hands | *47* |
| Zbig vs. Henry | *61* |
| If Not for Ford's Gaffe | *75* |
| Cuba for Hire | *83* |
| The Shah Checkmated | *95* |
| Hunting for Sparrows | *105* |
| Vienna 1979–Vienna 1959 | *123* |
| The Afghan Trap | *135* |
| Branded | *151* |
| Public Enemy # 1 | *163* |

## CONTENTS

| | |
|---|---:|
| Poland: 1980 and Afterward | *177* |
| Once Again, No Illusions | *187* |
| Second Chance | *201* |
| The New Chessboard | *215* |
| Bibliography | *227* |

# PREFACE
## SHLOMO AVINERI

Biographies of academics are a difficult genre, even when it comes to persons with a high public profile. Michael Ignatieff's *Isaiah Berlin—A Life*, and Adam Sisman's *An Honorable Englishman—The Life of Hugh Trevor-Roper*, wonderful as they both are, show the strains.

The Towers of Academe are constantly stormed by ambitious individual scholars, armed with footnotes adorning learned disputations: but then, as it has been said, the stakes are sometimes so small. No world historical battles, no decisions of life and death, no nail-biting moments of uncertainly on which hang the lives of millions. Another article, another symposium, a hard-won prestigious academic appointment, even a brilliant quip at High Table in All Souls don't equal the battle of Waterloo, the world historical consequences of the Ribbentrop-Molotov pact, or the agonizing debates of when and where to haunch the second front in World War II.

The same applies, albeit on a lesser key, to biographies of academics-turned-statesmen, as shown in Walter Isaacson's *Kissinger—A Biography*: for all its high dramatic moments, it has long stretches of less than exciting episodes. From the reader's point of

# PREFACE

view, policy position papers, sometimes written in Delphic academese, are a poor substitute for action.

Wisely, Andrzej Lubowski decided to follow a more eclectic approach. Rather than follow what would necessarily turn out to be a tedious account of academic and bureaucratic in-fighting and arcane arguments, sometimes couched in abstruse quasi-learned jargon, he chose to focus on a number of selected seminal issues addressed by Brzezinski during his career in the academy and in government. This is much more a biographical sketch than an overall detailed biography: yet by anchoring some chapters in quotes from Brzezinski's writings and interviews with him and other players, it is in a way following the revered English 19th-century tradition of "The Life and Times of … " genre. It is also more lively, and because it does not attempt to marshal all the evidence which could be found for or against a certain intellectual position or political move, it is also more open to challenge and controversy. Yet it captures most vividly and coherently both Brzezinski's personality as well the context of his writings and activities.

From his initial studies on totalitarianism, conducted with his Harvard mentor Carl J. Friedrich, Brzezinski's major concern has been the Soviet Union: its Marxist-Leninist ideology, its political system, its foreign policies, its expansion into Central Eastern Europe, its challenge to Western democracies and the Great Power competition which locked it into a global contest with American power and policies. His ability to combine geo-strategic thinking with a deep understanding of Russian history with its autocratic traditions and almost paranoid xenophobic approach to foreigners, endowed his writings, and later his policy recommendations, with unique insights mostly absent from the approaches of many US experts on the Soviet Union and international relations.

Because of this, Brzezinski's academic writings, his role in the Trilateral Commission and ultimately his position as National

## PREFACE

Security Adviser in the Carter Administration, necessarily beg the inevitable comparison with Henry Kissinger: that Brzezinski's time in office followed Kissinger's ascendancy in the Nixon and Ford Administrations—first as National Security Adviser and later as Secretary of State—brings the comparison even more into focus.

This fascinating juxtaposition of the two foreign-born persons so dominant for decades in formulating US foreign policy vis-à-vis the Soviet Union, naturally occupies a central place in Lubowski's account. Though it could be further nuanced, it brings out the clear contours of the major differences between the two. Both were ardently anti-communist and anti-Soviet, but for the sake of stability and fearful of a major World War II-like conflagration, Kissinger opted for a strategy of accommodation with Moscow, while Brzezinski, claiming that the very nature of Soviet ideology and policies prevents stability, sought strategies for undermining the Soviet system. In other words, Kissinger—with his Metternichian balance-of-power approach—was looking to anchor, through what would eventually be called detente, a status quo with the Soviet Union, while Brzezinski, with his somewhat Manichean mind-set, was aiming at radical, though controlled, change. Kissinger was for preserving the status quo, Brzezinski was for challenging it.

Hence their different approaches to issues of human rights: for all his commitment to democratic values, Kissinger viewed their use against the Soviet Union as a dangerous weapon, and shied away from them; Brzezinski, on the other hand, realized their usefulness as a wedge which could undermine the Soviet system from within without the use of overt Western force. Consequently, Brzezinski courted and encouraged dissidents in the Soviet Union and its satellites, while Kissinger avoided them and saw many of their activities as undermining the balance of power he had so assiduously crafted with the Kremlin. Without admitting it, Brzezinski was following some major facets of George Kennan's containment policies: this was the logic of "peaceful engagement."

## PREFACE

Brzezinski was also much more aware than Kissinger of the systemic weaknesses of the Soviet economy, which eventually contributed to Gorbachev's reform attempts and the system's eventual collapse.

In retrospect, Brzezinski was proven right and Kissinger was wrong. In the context of a study of Brzezinski, it may be unfair to focus on a "what if" scenario connected with Kissinger: but it surely is not wrong to see in President George H. W. Bush "Chicken Kiev" speech, as well as in Secretary of State James Baker's advise to the feuding last leaders of Yugoslavia to stick together rather than go their separate ways, echoes of Kissinger's fear of instability, chaos and unpredictability. In Kissinger's defense it should be stated that the steps leading to World War II gave him ample reasons for his preference for the status quo, even if problematical, over an unpredictable and unbridled series of changes which could lead to new catastrophes.

One of the reasons which helped Brzezinski in understanding the inner weakness and eventual brittleness of the Soviet system was his awareness of strong national undercurrents militating against Moscow's oppression—not only in the Warsaw Pact countries, forcibly incorporated into the Soviet system after 1945, but also within the multi-national Soviet Union itself. When in the White House he set himself up to foster these internal tensions.

Brzezinski's insistence in supporting Poland's Solidarność with its far-reaching potential of undermining the whole Soviet system was obvious. Brzezinski also grasped that part of this movement's subtext—and popularity—in Poland was not only its anti-communist, but also its anti-Russian and strongly Catholic agenda. Yet beyond this, Brzezinski was also right in seeing that with the onset of *perestroika*, not only democratic sentiments would be given relatively free reign, but also submerged national aspirations, as it happened in Georgia, Lithuania and other Soviet republics; given the Soviet Union's ostensibly federal system,

## PREFACE

the potential for a massive—and, paradoxically basically peaceful—breakup was evident. To Brzezinski, with *perestroika*, it was nationalism, as much as democratic aspirations, which eventually brought down the Soviet Union, the communist system and Soviet hegemony in Central Eastern Europe.

Lubowski rightly mentions how the Carter Administration's human rights policies, which Brzezinski helped to craft as a weapon against the Soviet Union, mobilized dissidents and undermined Moscow's oppressive system. Yet it should be recalled that these developments predated the Carter presidency and got much of their impetus from the 1975 Helsinki Final Act, signed during President Ford's administration.

The Helsinki Accords are an example of the dialectical tensions between intents and consequences. For Kissinger—then already Secretary of State—the Helsinki Final Acts were an instrument stabilizing post-1945 Europe. By accepting post-World War II borders (despite some Western reservations about the annexation of the Baltic states), and thus legitimizing the division of Germany, the US bound the Soviet Union to the acceptance of the principle of the inviolability of existing borders—for Kissinger a major guarantee for stability and the maintenance of status quo. Finally World War II came to an end with all parties accepting Europe's post-1945 map—so very different from the problematic nature of the Versailles Treaty.

Yet—and here lies the irony—by adding the Third Basket dealing with the preservation and promulgation of human rights and setting up a mechanism for their observance, the Helsinki Accords planted a time bomb under the Soviet Union. The Soviets agreed to the Third Basket as a sop to Western sensitivities, viewing it as empty language—much as similar language in the Soviet Constitution itself was mere empty phraseology. The Americans—and Kissinger—similarly viewed it as secondary to the epoch-making stabilizing factors of the major security baskets which were viewed as the core of the

## PREFACE

Accords. But the seed was sown, and the fact that so-called "Helsinki Committees" were established to monitor human rights issues, for the first time gave legitimacy to internal dissent and human rights issues in communist countries. This was a development the Soviets never thought would be brought into the world when they had signed the Accords, and which they rued ever after. When Carter and Brzezinski came into office, their insistence on issues of human rights was already anchored in international accords and institutional arrangements set up under Nixon-Ford and Kissinger.

The relationship between President Carter and Brzezinski as his National Security Adviser is spelt out by Lubowski is some detail, and Brzezinski's loyalty to his President is evident in this description as it is in his own memoirs. But the truth is that some of the grounds for criticism which would accompany Carter's foreign policy could be traced to that somewhat incongruous relationship.

They were indeed an odd couple: a provincial Southern governor, with little knowledge of the world outside the US and hardly any exposure to it, and a cosmopolitan, internationally well-connected sophisticated foreign affairs expert of Central European background, himself a scion of a diplomatic family.

Bringing together a born-again Christian, with basically pacifist premises, and a hard-bitten realist was obviously unusual. In theory, it could have been a mutually rewarding relationship, in which these two so different persons could have complemented each other and reap interesting results: but it was not to be. It is true that they were both committed to viewing human rights as an ingredient of foreign policy—but their approach differed. While Brzezinski believed human rights could be wrested from tyrannical regimes by using the big stick any US president was carrying, Carter seemed to believe they could be achieved by using his soft-spoken persuasive powers. Many years later, when he was already out of office, those who have met Carter in Jerusalem after his visits to Syria could not but be flummoxed by his paradoxical admiration

## PREFACE

for a strongman like Hafez Assad who he believed could be talked back into the path of righteousness.

Not surprisingly, it was Cyrus Vance, with his lawyerly approach and patience, who was much more in tune with Carter's reluctance to use even the faint threat of power—hence also his resignation after the failure of the Teheran embassy rescue operation. Eventually, Carter obviously changed course, but his newly found militancy lacked conviction and credibility; and in any case, it came too late. It is obvious from the book that Brzezinski would have preferred a much earlier tough stand, which might have made the later use of actual power superfluous.

Iran was indeed one of the major debacles of Carter's presidency. The failure to be even mildly aware of the tectonic undercurrents threatening the Shah's autocratic modernization project has to be credited to the ineptness of the American intelligence community, not to the White House. But Carter's preposterous statement in Teheran on New Year's Day 1978 that the Shah's Iran is "an island of stability in a turbulent region" would justly haunt his presidency as well as his historical legacy. Sadly, this might have been exacerbated by the White House's preoccupation at that time with Israeli-Arab relations: seeing the Arab-Israeli conflict as the only cause of instability in the region exerted its price in being less attentive than necessary to other facets of Middle Eastern developments.

Yet it is Afghanistan that Lubowski rightly identifies as the most problematic of the policies advocated and carried out by Brzezinski, and the context shows that here Brzezinski's finely tuned feel for the inner contradictions and weaknesses of the Soviet system has sometimes failed him. It is now fairly clear that the CIA operations against the Moscow-supported regime in Kabul precipitated the direct Soviet intervention in Afghanistan and can be viewed, in retrospect, as a not totally unjustified response to what the Kremlin viewed as an American provocation. Brzezinski, who

## PREFACE

was extremely careful in Europe not to cross the fine line between indirectly undermining Soviet power and directly confronting it, seems to have fewer compunctions in this regard when it came to far-away and not always well understood Afghanistan. To argue, as Brzezinski now does, that this after all drew Moscow into what eventually turned out to be one of its most catastrophic policy decisions which hastened the Soviet demise, is, of course, true: but this was not the intention of the decision to support the *mujahedins'* anti-communist guerilla and terrorists, even if it turned out to be one of the unintended consequences of this step.

But this is not the only instance of the cruel dialectics of unintended consequences. Lubowski deals fairly with the somewhat absurd allegation that by intervening in Afghanistan, the US "founded" Al Qaeda. Yet one cannot escape the conclusion that by encouraging the Islamist motivation of militarily opposing the Soviets (Carter in his condemnation of the Moscow's intervention even referred to the "atheistic" Soviet Union), it greatly helped turn anti-Western fundamentalist Islamicism from an ideology into an armed force.

It is also conceivable that the failure of the Teheran rescue mission helped galvanize a reluctant Carter to a more militant response to the Soviet direct military intervention in Afghanistan: the Soviet invasion has certainly been a deep shock for Carter and as he himself publicly admitted, helped change his mind about the nature of the Soviet system. Brzezinski's more assertive approach seemed to have trumped Carter's reluctance to the use of raw power. This was playing with fire—even if it can be persuasively argued that there were deeper causes for the rise of Islamist fundamentalism and its anti-Western radicalization would have taken place anyway. This policy also brought about, among other things, the murky connection between Al Qaeda (and the Taliban) and the Pakistani ISI security service which is still an enormous burden on US policy in the region, and will not easily go away.

## PREFACE

"Man is formed in the mold of his homeland" *(Ha-adam hu tavnit nof moladeto)*, wrote the Hebrew poet Shaul Tschernichovsky. Tschernichovsky, who died in Jerusalem in 1943, was born in the Crimea, and his poetry is deeply redolent with the sights and smells of his Russian and Ukrainian native vistas and evocative of associations far away from Judaism or the Land of Israel. With some exaggeration, he could even be called a Ukrainian poet writing in Hebrew.

There is no doubt that Brzezinski's Polish background has left its indelible mark on his worldview, despite the fact that—as Lubowski mentions—he had lived in Poland only a few years, and even that, when he was a very young child. Though it would be wrong to suggest—as some did—that his whole mindset, especially his views of the Soviet Union, Russia, and communism, were exclusively determined by his Polish Catholic origins, it cannot be denied that it was this background which shaped much of his view of the world. While always looking at US-Soviet relations from the strategic considerations of American interests and Western democratic values, it is obvious that looking at them from a window which virtually overlooked the Vistula gave him a different perspective—and sense of urgency—than if his sight would have been limited to overlooking the Hudson or the Potomac.

It is this window on the Vistula which added to Brzezinski's perspective an element of moral indignation, embedded in historical dimensions, which sometimes was lacking in the grand systemic strategic analyses of many American strategic experts. Brzezinski's factoring in of the moral dimension into his approach to the Soviet Union did not come from abstract—and therefore sometimes open to negotiations and thus diminution—theories of human rights, but from a deep and searing personal and historical experience which viewed Moscow not only as the capital of an imperial power using the ideology of world revolution for its expansionist politics, but also as the centuries'-old enemy and oppressor of

## PREFACE

the Polish nation. Hence the fire in his belly, which eventually was vindicated when the Soviet Union, and its empire, showed their signs of disintegration. It was Brzezinski's insight from the inside which enriched and strengthened Western strategies, and when the Kremlin lost its empire, many observes, who initially faulted Brzezinski for what they saw as an ethnocentrically driven set of prejudices, had to admit how right he had been all along.

It is this angle of vision which continues to inform Brzezinski's current skepticism of Russian policies under Putin and buttresses his fundamental doubts about the ability of Russia to proceed in the foreseeable future towards a consolidated democratic transition. It is for these reasons that Brzezinski seemed to have had fewer compunctions about US and NATO intervention against Serbia, and was furious with the Bush administration ultimate acquiescence with Russia's aggression against Georgia. All this also suggests that despite Brzezinski's basic support for the overall foreign policies of President Obama in a basically multi-polar world, on this issue he clearly differs from the latter's policy of "re-setting" relations with Moscow. It is a significant nuance.

When it comes to the Middle East, however, Brzezinski is much less sure-footed. The chapter on the region in this book deal much more with Brzezinski's current views on the Arab-Israeli conflict, including the Iran issue, than with the way in which he navigated US policy during his time in office. Hence some supplementary comments may be necessary.

Not surprisingly, Brzezinski has always tried to frame the Arab-Israeli conflict within the wider context of his global strategic vision. Yet this overall vision has sometimes made him less aware than necessary of the local, autochthonous, aspects of the conflict—and on this we have consistently held different views for a long time (see our exchange in *Foreign Policy*, Winter 1975-6).

During the Cold War, Brzezinski viewed the Middle East conflict as a derivative of the US-Soviet contest, and looked for

## PREFACE

ways to solve it through a grand deal with the Soviet Union. Currently, he views the conflict as a major obstacle to easing relations between the US and the Arab and Islamic world, and urgently urges an Israeli-Palestinian accommodation, to be accompanied by a muscular US leaning on Israel, so as to smooth US relations with the wider world of Islam. In both cases, there are aspects of the conflict which are indeed part of the wider horizons as Brzezinski views them—be it US-Soviet or US-Arab/Islamic. But the core of the conflict is a conflict between two national movements—the Jewish national movement as expressed by Zionism and the Palestinian, and wider Arab, national movement. It is the aspirations—and fears—of these two national movements that have to be addressed and a compromise between their conflicting claims that has to be achieved; absent such mutual, local understandings and agreements, merely strategic solutions coming from the outside will fail.

Such inattentiveness to the claims of local national players is somewhat surprising when it comes from a person as Brzezinski: as noted, one of his major intellectual and strategic achievements has been his realization that the Cold War cannot be viewed just as a Super Power contest and that one of the weaknesses of the Soviet Union—and one of the trump cards of the West—was the persistence and ultimate strength of the national consciousness of the peoples subjugated by the Soviet system, both within the USSR and in Central Eastern Europe. In the case of the Middle East, to overlook the strength of these sentiments, among Jews and Arabs alike, and pin one's hopes only on an accommodation of global strategic interests, is wrong for both intellectual and practical reasons.

Paradoxically, it was Kissinger who realized the intractability of trying to address the conflicting national claims in the Palestinian-Israeli conflict and therefore opted for a 'step by step' approach, while Brzezinski always preferred—and still prefers—the overall

## PREFACE

approach of a final status solution. Yet this approach has eluded until now both sides to the conflict—as well as numerous American presidents.

Let me reiterate what I stated to Lubowski—and to which he refers in the book—that it is utter nonsense to attribute Brzezinski's views on the Middle East conflict and Israel to some inbred anti-Semitism, supposedly coming from his Polish background. Such accusations, coming from some American Jewish leaders (less from Israel itself) are not only totally unfounded, but are also an evidence of total ignorance of Polish-Jewish relations in pre-World War II Poland and the way people of Brzezinski's personal and family background stood on these issues.

Lubowski's account of Brzezisnki's involvement in the Middle East peace process focuses naturally on his contacts with Prime Minister Menachem Begin during the negotiations following President Sadat's dramatic visit to Jerusalem. Yet during the first few months of Carter's presidency, the Israeli government was led by the Labor Party and Prime Minister Yitzhak Rabin. It is in this period that some wrong-footed steps taken by the White House helped undermine the credibility of the Rabin government and, paradoxically, helped to lead Begin's right-wing Likud to victory in the May 1977 elections.

This was obviously not the intention of either Carter or Brzezinski, but Brzezinski's move from Kissinger's careful step-by-step approach to a more ambitious comprehensive peace agreement had this effect. This was exacerbated by President Carter's March 16th, 1977 endorsement, at a town meeting in Clinton, Mass., of a Palestinian homeland. This was the first time an American president voiced such support for Palestinian statehood, which at that time was not the official position of the Israeli Labor-led government, which preferred the "Jordanian option." Carter's statement came a few days after Rabin's visit to the new president at the White House which was characterized by the press as somewhat tense,

## PREFACE

and it worked like a bombshell. By that time Israel was in the midst of an election campaign, and this was interpreted as a slap in the face of Rabin who always prided himself on close cooperation and understanding with the United States.

This public breach between Washington and Jerusalem was used by Begin's Likud opposition as an evidence of a major failure of Rabin's foreign policy, and put Labor on the defensive on this most sensitive issue of Israeli politics. It seems that the White House appeared to be totally unaware of the impact of such a presidential change of course on the heated politics of Israel.

A similar less than sure grip on Middle East realities was Brzezinski's initial response to President Sadat's initiative to visit Jerusalem in the fall of 1977, at that time with Begin already as Prime Minister. Following Brzezinski's views that peace in the region can be achieved through a concerted effort of the United States and the Soviet Union, Washington was involved in trying to move Moscow towards reviving the moribund Geneva Conference, jointly headed by the US and USSR. This has been a complete U-turn from post-1973 American policy, accepted by both Israel and Egypt, that the US should be the key player in peace making. Washington's surprising move was one of the reasons which caused Sadat—who had expelled Soviet advisers just a few years earlier, and did not want to see the return of Moscow to Middle East—to launch his visit to Jerusalem. When Sadat announced his move, Brzezinski appeared to fear that it might undermine his initiative for an international conference—which it actually did, but instead also led to successful bilateral Israeli-Egyptian negotiations and eventually to the first peace treaty between Israel and an Arab country. It is to Carter's White House credit that his administration very quickly shifted its position and recognized Sadat's initiative for what it really was—the most significant breakthrough in Middle East peace making in more than three decades. But initially, Sadat's bold initiative was not welcome in Washington.

## PREFACE

Echoes of this less than sure grip on Middle Eastern realities still seems to linger in some of Brzezinski's current approaches, as in his current belief that "there are indications that Iran is coming to resemble Turkey." Even those who agree with Brzezinski's recoiling from military action against Iran's nuclear program would be hard pressed to find proof that such a transformation is actually taking place in the Islamic Republic.

Let me end on a personal note.

As Andrzej Lubowski recounts in the book, Brzezinski visited Israel at my suggestion in June-July 1976 when he served as foreign policy adviser to presidential candidate Jimmy Carter. It so happened that the visit occurred during the tense week between the hijacking by Palestinian terrorists of an Air France airliner flying from Tel Aviv to Paris and the Israeli rescue operation which successfully freed the hostages held captive at Entebbe airport in Uganda, thousands of miles away from Israel.

One evening during that hectic week I hosted Brzezinski to a dinner party to which were invited a number of Israelis of Polish origin, among them the philosopher Nathan Rotenstreich, then Rector of the Hebrew University, whose father Ephraim Fiszel Rotenstreich had been a member of the Polish Sejm and later Senate in the 1920's. The conversation naturally drifted to Polish-Jewish relations between the two World Wars, and I used this occasion to present Brzezinski with a facsimile of the certificate of honor inscribing his father, the diplomat Tadeusz Brzezinski in the "Golden Book" of the Jewish National Fund in Jerusalem in the 1930's. The certificate was accompanied by a citation by the "Polish Jewish Community in Leipzig" in recognition of Consul Brzezinski's help to members of their community. At that time there were quite a number of Jews of Polish origin who fled to Germany in World War I from the war

## PREFACE

zones in the east, but many of them did not have any valid citizenship papers, either German or Polish. They were among the first Jews persecuted by the Nazis because of their unclear status, and lacking any papers they were in an impossible situation, not being able to apply for immigration anywhere. They approached the Polish consular officials in Leipzig, and Brzezinski Sr. provided them with passports and travel documents, even though in many cases they were not strictly entitled to them: but they could now at least try to apply for immigration and thus be saved from Nazi persecution.

Zbig is not known as an emotional person and he certainly does not wear his feelings on his sleeve. This was, however, the only instance in which I saw him deeply moved, and I don't think I imagined seeing his eyes soften from their usual hard look. In thanking me, Zbig added that during the previous days, when the whole country was worrying about the fate of the abducted Israelis on the Air France plane, he learned something about Jewish solidarity: nowhere else would the whole business of the country come to a virtual standstill in case of a similar hijacking. I could see how this feeling of community—in the 1930's and now in 1976—spoke to Zbig's Polish notion of patriotism and national responsibility.

Some time before that memorable dinner, a left-wing kibbutz-based publishing house in Tel Aviv, *Sifriat Poalim* ("Workmen's Library"), asked me to edit a Hebrew collection of Brzezinski's essays on international affairs and write an introduction to the volume. When I asked the publisher, David Hanegbi, who years earlier had edited the Hebrew version of the standard Soviet edition of Marx's and Engels' *Selected Works*, why they would be interested in publishing a volume by a person not exactly known for his sympathy to the Soviet Union, he looked at me with the sad eyes of a

# PREFACE

disillusioned former Soviet sympathizer, dismissing my query with the curt reply: "It doesn't matter. He knows Russia and understands Soviet policy."

Brzezinski could probably not expect a more incongruous yet telling compliment than this one coming from an elderly kibbutznik in the remote Valley of Jezreel in northern Israel. Similarly, and much more importantly, Lubowski's book will now undoubtedly help render to Brzezinski the recognition due to him for the crucial role he played, as academic and policy-maker, in promoting peacefully but powerfully one of the major transformational developments which helped usher in the 21st century.

Shlomo Avineri is Professor of Political Science at the Hebrew University of Jerusalem and member of the Israel Academy of Sciences and Humanities. He served as Director-General of Israel's Ministry of Foreign Affairs in the first cabinet of Prime Minister Yitzhak Rabin. His books, which have been translated into many languages, include *The Social and Political Thought of Karl Marx*, *Hegel's Theory of the Modern State*, *Israel and the Palestinians*, *The Making of Modern Zionism* and (with Zeev Sternhell) *Europe's Century of Discontent: The Legacies of Fascism, Nazism and Communism*.

# ZBIG

## THE MAN WHO CRACKED THE KREMLIN

# PROLOGUE

The Vatican, October 1978. Pope John Paul II, grinning mischievously from ear to ear, says "Thank you, Professor. I understand that I owe my job at the Holy See to you." Brzezinski chuckles along. Karol Wojtyła is alluding openly to the theory propagated by Moscow that the election of a Polish pope was no accident, that Washington influenced the decision that the cardinals made in conclave because it saw a Polish pope as an instrument for combating the Soviets, that the CIA lent history a helping hand.

Brzezinski recalls that exchange with a touch of emotion, but he cannot suppress a guffaw. This new conspiracy theory was either a product of paranoia or merely one of many attempts to hoodwink the world. Nevertheless, as life would prove, the fact that both the head of the powerful Catholic Church and the adviser to the president of the mightiest country in the world had been born in Poland was not without significance for the rebellion of Polish workers against communist tyranny.

Several months later, Deng Xiaoping, the de facto leader of China after the death of Mao, barely had time to unpack in Blair House before setting out for his first supper in America, at the Brzezinski home. The children of the adviser to President Carter acted as servers and the menu was American, but afterwards the host served Russian vodka, a present from Soviet ambassador Dobrynin. The communist heretic got a kick out of hearing Brzezinski remark that they were having Brezhnev's favorite drink.

Brzezinski was not yet thirty when he served as an advisor to John F. Kennedy. Half a century later, it was Obama. In the meantime, he taught at prestigious universities while writing more than a dozen books and hundreds of articles. He arouses strong feelings, from adoration to outright hatred, but no one is neutral about him. He became the focus of conspiracy theories and every conceivable label was hung on him. For some he is the latest incarnation of Rasputin, and for others a dangerous freemason or a Doctor Strangelove. Yet others see him as the godfather of Al Qaeda. In a word, he is notorious. This is a lot for one man. I found him intriguing long ago, and still do. That is why I wrote this book. It is neither a classical biography nor a detailed scholarly analysis, although it contains a dash of the one and the other. Its subject is a man's life and views.

This young boy from Warsaw, Poland, was stranded on distant shores by the war. Eleven years old and in Canada when Hitler attacked Poland, he spent no more than three years in the country of his parents. How, less than two decades later, did he come to analyze the world in a way that grabbed the attention of Washington? At least six presidents of the United States sought his advice in more or less formal ways. How did he end up where he ended up? The fact that America is a wide-open country hardly means that it is easy to reach the corridors of power, or that people who make it into those corridors find it easy to avoid stumbling and being quickly shown the exit.

I am holding a dog-eared book in my hands: *Totalitarian Dictatorship and Autocracy* by Carl J. Friedrich and Zbigniew Brzezinski. I read in the introduction to the first edition, printed in 1955—Brzezinski was 27—that it is the outcome of work in a Harvard seminar, a seminar that Brzezinski joined in 1951, when he was 23.

# ZBIG

— ★ —

More than sixty years have passed since then. At the end of January 2011, Egypt was in turmoil, plunged into a revolt against tyranny. Christiane Amanpour was preparing her Sunday program on ABC. Who could explain to America what was happening in Cairo? Amanpour, like other leading TV journalists from the American networks, the BBC, and Al Jazeera, turned to one man. On Sunday, January 30, 2011, America listened to Zbigniew Brzezinski.

A distinguished gentleman who hardly looks his age, he has the springy step, the penetrating gaze, and the strong voice, energy, and drive of a man fifteen years younger. Among people I talked to about Brzezinski, I sensed more respect than affection. The reason for this is straightforward. His exceptional self-assurance, unrelenting logic, high expectations of others, and low tolerance for vapidity, hot air, and hypocrisy—none of which are in short supply on all sides—long ago earned him a reputation for arrogance that he has never lost. He never pretends to be less than he is. He browbeats people readily. He has never cozied up to the media—an offense for which the penalties are harsh in Washington. He does not mince words when an interviewer reveals ignorance, and he turns down interviews on trite subjects. This is a good way to come across as conceited.

Until the last meeting my hero seemed icily cold. He was always impeccably elegant when I met him. Those meetings were brief but meaty, and we always spoke English. Only when I went to see him one last time, in July 2011, did a different side of the man come out. The heat in Washington was stifling and the professor appeared in his office in a linen sports jacket, with no tie. I sat in the adjacent room poring over his correspondence with President Carter. He looked in from time to time to ask if anything needed explaining, and then just after noon he suggested that we have lunch in a nearby Greek restaurant. It was getting cloudy, so I asked if I should take my umbrella. "*Ma Pan parasol?*" he asked in Polish—do you have an umbrella? Yes, I replied, and he said "*To byczo.*"

I hadn't heard the word *byczo* for a long time. It was like someone exclaiming "that's tip-top" in English; it tickled me and I complemented him on his Polish vocabulary. Brzezinski's English is highly resourceful and almost surgically precise, but in Polish he comes across as less hard-edged, and just a touch saucy. It is like the difference between a crunchy apple and a succulent pear. At table, the harsh professor changed into a charming companion in conversation. Out came the anecdotes, the jokes, and the telling reminiscences. At first I tried to draw him out, but at a certain point I no longer needed to do so. When I asked about Gorbachev, he recalled meeting him in Paris a few years earlier. They had both been invited to address the French parliament. While Brzezinski was checking in he heard a drawn-out salutation from across the hotel lobby: "Zbi-i-i-g, Zbi-i-i-i-g." Brzezinski told me that was how his Russian acquaintances addressed him. He looked around. A few meters behind him stood the beaming Gorbachev. They greeted each other warmly, almost like old friends. In the French senate a day later, Brzezinski spoke first. Gorbachev followed him onto the podium and, to Zbig's surprise, launched a merciless attack on him in rhetoric harking back to the old Soviet days. "Not everyone, it is clear, finds the end of the Cold War to their liking," Gorbachev thundered, nodding in Brzezinski's direction. "I was flabbergasted," my interlocutor related over his tzatziki, "and when the gala session adjourned I went up and asked what had gotten into him and why he had said the things he said. Gorbachev smiled broadly and said, 'Zbig, they paid you and they paid me, and they want a little bit of conflict.'"

Recounting his next meeting with Gorbachev, Zbig noted that on that occasion he was the one who behaved less than elegantly. In Berlin for the anniversary of the tearing down of the wall, he once again heard the familiar call of "Zbi-i-i-i-g" while checking in at the hotel. Gorbachev, wearing a long leather jacket, was standing not far away. "I went up to him and said, 'Mikhail, you look like a Cheka agent.' That was out of place, I admit."

I was starting to understand something that Maria Smith, the wife of our mutual friend Gen. William Y. Smith, USAF (Ret), had once told me. She talked about Brzezinski's habit, during their frequent suppers together, of being provocative. He loved the clash of verbal swords and often tried to enliven the conversation by taking positions contrary to his own views and then defending them energetically. It was surrogate fencing, logical rivalry. The supper table stood in for the tennis court. He still played tennis regularly, several times a week. For my part, I had developed tennis elbow from banging away at the computer keyboard a dozen or more hours a day. I mentioned this when we were walking back to the office. Zbig halted in the middle of the busy sidewalk and began demonstrating an exercise routine that should help me.

The word in Washington—always behind his back and never to his face—is that his views and politics result from his Polish roots, that, as a Pole, he is a Russophobe and anti-Semite. Zbig understood better than most the essence of Soviet totalitarianism and the subsequent re-emergence of Russian imperial longings. He saw the former as a threat to world democracy, liberty, and freedom. Post-Soviet policy in its Putin variant strikes him as a danger to Russia's neighbors as well as to the budding aspirations and longings for liberty of the Russians themselves. For a long time he has been one of the few to openly criticize the role the pro-Israel lobby plays in shaping both American foreign policy and, not infrequently, the policies of Israel itself. That takes more than a little courage, a quality Brzezinski does not lack. Nor did he lack courage when he was one of the few members of the so-called Establishment to criticize sharply the policies of the nation's leader in a time of war, George W. Bush.

He is a scholar, strategist, teacher, and man of courage—but no saint. He has his faults. He has made mistakes. In the book, I attempt to define who Zbig is, what he believes in, what makes him different from other architects of superpower policy.

"No one understands the interdependence of power and principle better than Zbigniew Brzezinski" writes Jimmy Carter on the cover of his former national security adviser's *Second Chance: Three Presidents and the Crisis of American Superpower*.

Brzezinski believes, and has always believed, that values are important. He remained fiercely loyal to Carter above all, I think, because he respected President Carter's deep commitment to values. He defended Carter when others had loosed the hounds on him.

What would have happened if President Gerald R. Ford had not committed the monumental gaffe during a televised debate in San Francisco that surely cost the incumbent the 1976 election? The legendary Henry Kissinger would have remained the architect of American foreign policy. What is the difference between Brzezinski and Kissinger?

Is Brzezinski, the one-time chairman of the Trilateral Commission, a tool of the powerful or a defender of human rights? Could he be both?

Why did Deng Xiaoping, who roused China from lethargy and pushed it onto the road of modernization at a breakneck pace, get along better with Brzezinski than almost any other significant Western figure? When Brzezinski was in the White House and when he had left, Deng was always eager to see him.

A part of Washington saw Brzezinski as a schemer driven by megalomania. The Kremlin saw him as its most dangerous adversary.

The more time I spent combing the archives, the more I read, the more firmly convinced I became that the status of public enemy number one, which the Kremlin reserved for Brzezinski over the course of many long years, was more than a symptom of an obsession. There was something to it. Brzezinski did indeed play an underappreciated role in the unexpectedly rapid demise of the USSR. He saw the cracks in the facade of the Soviet system more clearly and forecast its ultimate downfall earlier than anyone else in the Washington establishment. When he found himself in the White House he architected the policies that contributed to the erosion and ultimate collapse of the Soviet Union.

# FREE OF ILLUSIONS

**When Ukrainian children played a game of chance called "lottery," they shouted "Holodomor!" whenever 33 came up. The term denotes the horrific starvation associated with the year 1933 (although it began in 1932), during which nearly seven million people died as a result of forced collectivization.**

Tadeusz Brzezinski, a veteran of the Polish-Bolshevik War and later consul in France and Germany, was named Polish consul general in Kharkiv, Ukraine, in 1936. He did not take his family to his new posting. He was well aware of what was happening there at the time. On a visit to Warsaw, he told about how his acquaintances were disappearing on a mass scale, without a trace. Almost twenty years later his son, Zbigniew, would write his doctoral dissertation at Harvard on *The Role of the Purge in the Totalitarian State*.

Tadeusz Brzezinski returned to Warsaw the following year. In the fall, he took up the post of consul general in Montreal. His son enrolled in school there and took Russian lessons. In May 1939, Polish foreign minister Jozef Beck responded to Hitler's repudiation of the German-Polish non-aggression by reassuring an enthusiastic Sejm—the parliament—that the Polish army "will refuse to surrender not only the overcoat, but even a button from that overcoat." When the war started, Zbig—eleven years old and far from Poland—believed that the conflict would be brief and the aggressor punished, with the soldiers whose parades he had watched with feelings of pride and joy triumphant. How was he to know that those splendid warriors on horseback stood no chance against Hitler's tanks? He vigilantly followed the dispatches from the combat zone and drew lines on maps. He began to understand that the fate of his country and the fate of the whole world depended on things happening far from Montreal. He received bitterly the news from the 1943 Teheran conference that Roosevelt and Churchill had caved in to Stalin over Poland's postwar borders. The outraged fifteen-year-old Brzezinski even wrote a letter to Churchill and enclosed a map showing the 1939 borders.

That same year, he learned that the mass graves of Polish officers had been unearthed near Katyn. He had no doubts as to the identity of the perpetrators. In 1989, with the consent of Gorbachev's government, he laid a wreath on their burial place.

Later, in *The Grand Failure*, Brzezinski wrote that

> *The titanic war later waged between Hitler's Nazi Germany and Stalin's Soviet Russia has made many forget that the struggle between them was a fratricidal war between two strands of a common faith. To be sure, one proclaimed itself to be unalterably opposed to Marxism and preached unprecedented racial hatred: and the other saw itself as the only true offspring of Marxism in practicing unprecedented class hatred. But both elevated the State into the highest organ of collective action, both used brutal terror as the means of exacting social obedience, and both engaged in mass murders without parallel in human history. Both also organized their social control by similar means, ranging from youth groups to neighborhood informers to centralized and totally censored means of mass communications. And, finally, both asserted that they were engaged in constructing all-powerful "socialist" states.*
>
> *It is relevant to note that Hitler was an avid student of the practices initiated both by Lenin and Mussolini. These two*

*men were his precursors, especially in regard to the use of new means of communications in energizing and then in mobilizing the newly politically awakened masses. But all three were pioneers in the quest for total power, and they were extraordinarily skillful in blending the exploitation of political passion with disciplined political organization. . . .*

*Moreover, with the passage of time each side came to embrace the other's major themes and even symbols. During World War II, Stalin increasingly legitimized his new ruling class with nationalist slogans, by pretentious uniforms even for his civilian bureaucrats, and through an exaltation of Great Power highly reminiscent of Nazi practices. Hitler at time remarked that while Stalin was a "beast," the Soviet dictator was at least a beast "on a grand scale," that Stalin was a "fellow of genius" for whom one had to have "unreserved respect," and that with another ten to fifteen years in power he would make the Soviet Union "the greatest power in the world."*

*After the abortive coup against Hitler in 1944, the Nazi regime justified the extermination of the German aristocracy in a language of class hatred indistinguishable from the Soviet Union's. Hitler even exhibited a perverse envy of Stalin, who had taken Leninism to its logical conclusion. "I have bitterly regretted" he said, "that I did not purge my officer corps in the way Stalin did."*

Brzezinski was seventeen when the war ended. There was no future in the new Poland for a diplomat from the prewar government—especially one who had spent the war next door to America—nor for his children. Zbig, as he would soon come to be known forever more, found himself at McGill University in Montreal. When he studied Russia and read about the atrocities, it was more than a distant echo. His M.A. thesis was titled "Russian-

Soviet Nationalism." As opposed to other noted Kremlinologists, Brzezinski always knew that the Soviet Union was no monolith, and that ethnic problems were one of the main weaknesses of the Soviet superpower.

Not for a moment did he entertain any illusions as to the nature of the Soviet system. Nor, however, did he ever underestimate it. The communists were not more likely to behave irrationally than their more pragmatic Western adversaries, particularly the Anglo-Saxons. As he wrote in the introduction to his 1961 book *Ideology and Power in Soviet Politics*, "for example, Suez in 1956 and Cuba in 1961 provide good illustrations of desperation and impatience leading into what might be appropriately described as irrational conduct. In both cases, the chief Western errors were failures of theoretical and ideological omission, and from them followed the military and logistical inadequacies." In Brzezinski's view, "the theoretical error involved the failure to perceive that in Nasser and in Castro one was dealing no longer with a traditional-type system that could be overthrown from within by the application of merely limited external forces. Both leaders have successfully eliminated intermediary social groups and skillfully mobilized the masses. What is the political nature of our opponent? That question was either not raised or inadequately answered."

The essay "Totalitarianism and Rationality," first published in 1956, when the author was 28, starts with a definition of totalitarianism.

> *What is distinctively new about it? Certainly, autocratic systems in the past displayed many of the features developed and accentuated by modern totalitarianism. Diocletian's tyranny or the Shogunate in Japan, for instance, stressed to a high degree the acquiescence of the population in central-*

> ized control. Both systems also institutionalized an atmosphere of fear through a system of secret police informers not unlike the totalitarian societies of the twentieth century. Similarly, we find among many of the nineteenth-century European reformers a readiness to use violence for the sake of postulated improvements and reforms like the ideological intolerance and consequent brutality of the Rosenbergs of Zhdanovs of our age. Cromwell's regime also displayed some analogies. . . .
>
> Unlike most dictatorships of the past and present, the totalitarian movements wielding power do not aim to freeze society in the status quo: on the contrary, their aim is to institutionalize a revolution that mounts in scope, and frequently in intensity, as the regime stabilizes itself in power.

"An average Hungarian under Horthy or a Frenchman under Louis XIV was not directly drawn into the operations of the regime and could continue in his traditional associations much as before the advent of the ruler. The ruler himself based his power to a great extent on the varying alliances reached among combinations of socio-political forces and maintained in power as long as such alliances endured. Revolutionary changes were hence anathema to a dictatorship of this kind," writes Brzezinski. "It is only totalitarianism of our age that rejects all three kinds of restraints. It not only subverts the direct restrains immediately after the seizure of power but, unlike traditional dictatorships, it proceeds, once entrenched, to destroy all existing associations in society in order to remake that society, and subsequently, even man himself, according to certain 'ideal' conceptions."

Carl J. Friedrich, Brzezinski's teacher and mentor at Harvard, a pioneer in the study of totalitarianism who co-authored his student's *Totalitarian Dictatorship and Autocracy*, defines totalitarianism as a syndrome encompassing an official ideology, a single mass party, a technologically conditioned near-complete monopoly of all means of effective armed combat and of effective mass communication, and a system of terroristic police control. Brzezinski added to this definition a critical element that specifies the essence of the system: an articulated goal. What is the purpose of it all? Its purpose is institutionalized revolutionary fanaticism.

The essay "The Nature of the Soviet System," published in 1961, uses as its motto a quote from Andre Gide: "If the mind is obligated to obey the word of command, it can at any rate feel that it is not free. But if it has been so manipulated beforehand that it obeys without even waiting for the word of command, it loses even the consciousness of enslavement."

Gide paints a particularly grim picture of a society where it is not the rulers who anticipate the reactions of society and try to manipulate them, but rather the masses who anticipate the desires of the rulers and attempt to adapt to them.

Brzezinski was sometimes amused but more frequently irritated by the astonishing cocktail of ignorance and wishful thinking that characterized the West's reaction to personnel changes in the East, and especially the Soviet Union. When a Kremlin coup stripped Khrushchev of power in 1964, the American press churned out stories about how the bumptious Nikita who banged his shoe at the UN was being replaced by people in impeccably tailored suits. When the Brezhnev-Kosygin duo succeeded Khrushchev, *Newsweek* gushed in a November 26, 1964 article titled "Two for One" about how handsome Brezhnev was, how he was obviously a former athlete, how elegantly he dressed in Italian ties and silk shirts, and how he hunted, swam, and rooted for a soccer team. He was a collector of antique watches and an amateur ornithologist. He doted over his daughter Galina, who dreamed of becoming a film star. His kissing the hand of Frau Ulbricht, wife of the East German communist boss, exemplified his irreproachable manners. He was neither as impulsive as Khrushchev nor as loose-lipped. An analytical pragmatist, he based his decisions—as befitted an engineer—on facts rather than speculation. It was indeed noted that he was not averse to having a drink, but how much of a fault was that, especially in the Kremlin? He could hardly be criticized for the degree to which his taste and lifestyle had evolved from his proletarian roots. Experiences change people. Far more important was his authority over the army, from which he retired with the rank of major general despite never having led soldiers in combat. This authority had sufficed to quell the army in 1957 when Khrushchev cashiered Marshal Zhukov, the war hero who rode a white charger into Red Square to inspect the troops during the 1945 victory parade. After insisting on sending the army into Budapest in 1956 and backing Khrushchev in the 1957 showdown with the Molotov faction, Zhukov broke ranks over differences on military policy. Nikita demonstrated that he and he alone ruled the party, but Brezhnev was instrumental in helping him carry the day. Khrushchev repaid the favor by elevating Brezhnev to the post of titular president, as Chairman of the Supreme Soviet. The Kremlinology cottage industry had a much less colorful palette to use in the portrait of Kosygin, who thus figured, as *Newsweek* saw things in 1964, as "a solid man." This "solid man" had been deputy chairman of the Council of People's Commissars from 1940 to 1946 and a member of the Politburo from 1946—through seven years of Stalin's rule. His qualifications must therefore have somewhat exceeded the technocratic role that the American press attributed to him.

Brzezinski was more interested in the views and methods of the new Kremlin overlords than in their suits and ties. He was not seduced by ornithology, a beloved daughter, or mulling over whether it was Kosygin's innate affability that protected him from the Stalinist purges that ground up and spat out the Leningrad party elite in the late thirties. The changing of the Kremlin guard evoked neither euphoria nor hope in Brzezinski. In response to the mirage of modernization being fed to the average American, he wrote in the November 14, 1964 *New Republic*, shortly after the coup, about the triumph of aparatchiks and "bureaucratic mediocrities" who kept their heads above water when Stalin was conducting his mass purges. Brzezinski stated that the rulers of the Soviet Union had reached the summit through a process of negative selection, and that this method of choosing the leadership augured nothing good for the country.

In *The Great Failure*, Brzezinski wrote that, despite being accompanied at the outset by slogans about modernization, Brezhnev's rule amounted in practice to the restoration of quasi-Stalinism, guided by a desire to re-establish a certain fundamental order after the tempestuous reforms of Khrushchev. . . . Earlier, the mortar holding society together had been the Patriotic War for biological survival, followed by the necessity of rising up from the ruins. Now there was no such mortar. Mass terror may indeed have ended, but not arbitrary political coercion.

Brzezinski wrote in *The Grand Failure* that

> *The Stalinist system endured not only because Brezhnev and his immediate comrades benefited from it and remained loyal to it. It survived because it had become a vast structure of overlapping privileges, controls, rewards, and vested interests. It also endured because the newly urbanized Soviet masses could not conceive of any other alternative, having been for half a century inculcated with the notion that their experience represented for them a giant step forward. . . . The society as a whole was politicized from the top down, but real politics was confined only to the very top. The system was thereby protected from the challenge of change, but stagnation was the inevitable price of the system's coercive self-perpetuation.*

Brzezinski contrasted the historical pessimism of the Brezhnev-era Soviet elite with the gloating optimism of Khrushchev, who talked on every possible occasion about how the USSR would soon "bury" America in the economic race. Khrushchev did not do this out of simple bravado. Calculations by Soviet planners stood behind his certitude. The people believed that things were getting better. Successful atomic bomb tests followed by the flights of Sputnik and Gagarin boosted the faith. Later, such booster shots were in short supply. From time to time there were cheering stumbles by the rival, from race riots to recession, inflation, and finally the Watergate scandal, that the Kremlin interpreted as expressions of American weakness. None of this, however, could blind the average Soviet citizen to the lack of basic consumer goods or the sharing of apartments by several families, but political jokes were best confined to circles of trusted friends. Neither the ubiquitous shortages nor the fear had vanished.

Brzezinski made the point in *The Great Failure* that Gorbachev's emergence was no caprice of history. Given the deep crisis, if there had been no Gorbachev, then some other reformer would have come along in the mid-eighties. Zbig empathized with Gorbachev but realized at the same time that he faced the task of squaring the circle. It was easier to talk about *perestroika* and *glasnost* than to answer the question of what to do with Leninism.

He showed that the catastrophe was approaching so rapidly that even anti-reformers felt the need for a modicum of liberalization. The question was how far-reaching it should be, and how it should be introduced: In the "Leninist" top-down style favored by party hardliners, or through democratization, as Gorbachev's instincts prompted him. To show the difference between these two approaches, Brzezinski turned in *The Great Failure* to the words of Aleksander Gelman, a Russian playwright and screenwriter who fervently supported Gorbachev and said several years before the collapse that

## ANDRZEJ LUBOWSKI

> *"Democratization provides for the redistribution of power, rights, and freedoms, the creation of number of independent structures of management and information. And liberalization is the conservation of all the foundations of the administrative system but in milder form. Liberalization is an unclenched fist, but the hand is still the same and at any moment it could be clenched again into a fist."*

"Perestroika is our last chance," said Gorbachev on January 8, 1988. "If we stop, it will be our death."

Death came more quickly than anyone expected. Its arrival was speeded by the processes Zbig had written his M.A. thesis about in Canada in 1949, and to which he devoted a major part of his academic and political life—namely, ethnic conflicts. The public denunciation of Stalinism made possible by glasnost became a convenient form of camouflage for manifesting anti-Russian sentiments. Without pointing the finger at the Russians, a Ukrainian writer could condemn Stalin as a criminal for killing off the Ukrainian cultural elite and starving millions of Ukrainians to death. Balts could assemble to commemorate the victims of Stalinist deportation and demand greater autonomy without blaming the Russians. Tatars could protest against their exile and Muslims could organize pilgrimages to the graves of their mullahs. Gorbachev could not go on talking about glasnost if he banned such demonstrations. The scale of them shocked a Kremlin that was cut off from reality and had been lulled for decades by rhetoric about a united nation.

On top of all this came the tragedy of Afghanistan with its costs in blood, fortune, credibility, and morale, and the rapid splitting at the seams of communist domination in the European countries of the Soviet bloc. The illusions were bursting like soap bubbles. Brzezinski had never been taken in by them.

— ★ —

## Notes

On Hitler and Stalin, *The Grand Failure*, pp. 6-8.

On Suez and Cuba, *Ideology and Power in Soviet Politics* pp. 6-7.

For the definition of totalitarianism, *Ibid.*, pp. 14-15.

"An average Hungarian . . . ," *Ibid.*, pp. 17-18.

Gide quote, *Ibid.*, p. 65.

The survival of the Stalinist system, *The Grand Failure*, pp. 33-34.

Gelman quote, *Ibid.*, pp. 45-46.

Gorbachev quote, *Ibid.*, pp. 53.

# FROM KENNEDY TO ROCKEFELLER

"America is a place where a man called Zbigniew Brzezinski can make a name for himself without even changing it" was a wisecrack cherished by Zbig's friends, as Brzezinski began to climb the ladder of fame and respect.

Zbig enjoyed his academic success but never felt the allure of a lifetime spent as a venerable lecturer strolling in a tweed jacket across the yards of august campuses. He wanted to make himself count for something, and that meant policymaking. Doing so unaffiliated and at his own expense was difficult if for no other reason than until 1958 he did not hold American citizenship. A better way of making an impact on reality was to use people who had already made names for themselves, and who possessed the funds and contacts he lacked, as vehicles for his own concepts. A young senator from Massachusetts fit the bill. The fact that both Zbig and his wife Muszka simply liked Kennedy was an additional plus.

Brzezinski was so brimful of ideas that he had no need of custom tailoring them to Kennedy's requirements. From the moment the Soviets got the bomb—"Joe-3" was how the Americans referred to the Russian device dropped from an altitude of 33,000 feet in October 1951, when Zbig was at Harvard—the rivalry took on a new meaning. Armed conflict risked mutual destruction. Dropping out of the race and totally isolating the communist world like some leper colony would sentence the nations under Soviet occupation to slavery with no prospect of ever ending. The alternative, in Brzezinski's view, was an approach that he called "peaceful engagement." We wouldn't slam the door on them; we would try to open them up. We had more to gain than to lose. He knew that it would be a long, wearisome process. Kennedy liked the idea. It was fresh, stimulating, and, as the young senator saw it, promising.

John Fitzgerald Kennedy sent the 29-year-old Brzezinski a letter in August 1957 that is now held in the archives of the Library of Congress. After thanking Brzezinski for his help in preparing a speech about Poland that Kennedy delivered on the Senate floor, it expresses the hope that Brzezinski approved of the text.

In his Senate speech of August 21, Kennedy proposed lifting restrictions on aid to Poland and other Soviet bloc countries. He had signaled this idea earlier, in a message that his sister, Eunice Shriver, conveyed to an audience in Chicago: "We could help these countries which are not now fully Communistic or which are not now fully free. In this manner we can carve more elastic tools to work with in situations such as the one that occurred in Poland after 1956."

That same month, Zbig set foot on native soil for the first time since leaving Poland as a child. The visit reaffirmed his conviction that the evolution of the system, all its imperfections notwithstanding, was a better solution than spontaneous outbursts doomed to failure and reprisals.

The West speculated that communism was already a little bit different, more open, after the Twentieth Congress of the CPSU and Khrushchev's "revelations." The "sensational" speech, the first open condemnation of Stalin's methods, contained nothing that came as a sensation to Brzezinski, who had no illusions about the nature of the system. He regarded Khrushchev's call for a return to "Leninist roots" as a rotten prescription, because he believed that the whole problem lay precisely in those Leninist roots. While other

Kremlinologists got wound up over the "breakthrough," Brzezinski maintained an attitude of restraint.

Zbig took a look at Khrushchev and a look at Mao. He wondered what that Chinese-Soviet alliance was really like. Was it natural? Did the exalted phrases camouflage conflict? On June 11, 1956, *The New Republic* carried Brzezinski's article "Shifts in the Satellites," which the 28-year-old author had submitted under the title "Stalinism and the Satellites." It talked about the ripening differences within the Soviet camp, about emerging conflicts and Moscow's dilemmas: On how long a leash should the satellite regimes be held? How much autonomy should they be permitted?

Brzezinski's theses were controversial. The rout of the Hungarian uprising and the disappointment of the Polish October thaw were interpreted as proof that unity was prevailing over conflicts. Questions were also raised about the hypothetical Soviet-Chinese conflict to which Zbig devoted a great deal of space, regarding it as a process of historical significance.

In his 1960 presidential campaign, Kennedy frequently drew on Zbig's thinking. On October 1, 1960, the *New York Times* reported that the candidate was calling for the use of United States economic and moral power to implement a policy of "patiently encouraging freedom and carefully pressuring tyranny." It went on to quote Senator Kennedy:

> *We do not want to mislead the people of Poland or Hungary again that the United States is prepared to liberate them. We have no right, unless we are prepared to meet our commitments, to incite them to national suicide. But neither should the United States leave them without hope.*

Like his wife, Brzezinski joined the campaign effort. His role was modest despite the fact that the press got carried away and referred to him as the head of Kennedy's foreign-policy advisors. He took satisfaction in the presence of people he knew and respected in the new president's entourage. McGeorge Bundy, Zbig's dean of faculty at Harvard, became the president's advisor for national security affairs. Kennedy named Gen. Maxwell Taylor first his personal advisor on military affairs and then chairman of the Joint Chiefs of Staff. Taylor's assistant, in turn, was William Y. Smith, an Air Force officer wounded on his 97th sortie in Korea who was doing a PhD at Harvard, and whose wife was a close friend of Muszka's. Later, as Gen. W. Y. Smith, he served as deputy commander of the American armed forces in Europe. It was at his home that I met Brzezinski, and it was from him and Maria Smith that I heard about a Brzezinski who was warm, friendly, and witty—not only arrogant, obsessive, and conceited, which was how American journalists described him to me.

In February 1960, Harvard University Press published his book *The Soviet Bloc: Unity and Conflict*. It made a splash in the academic world and enhanced the still young political scientist's standing. For thirty years it was a college textbook that never went out of date. Radio Free Europe read excerpts on the air. It was published in *samizdat* inside the Soviet Union. After that empire fell, *Foreign Affairs* (September-October 1997) listed *The Soviet Bloc: Unity and Conflict* among "the most important books of the last seventy-five years."

Like everything Zbig wrote, this was not a work filled with elegant models, but rather a compendium of theory with recommendations in the sphere of real policy. America sent the iron-curtain countries false signals, harming those countries and itself. It made painful, costly mistakes. Declarations about exalted goals aren't worth much without the corresponding deeds. Responsibility and reason urge a different course. Zbig suggested a more subtle approach of going halfway to meet communist countries desirous of being less dependent on Moscow, even if that meant backing those countries' governments—a policy of "driving wedges" instead of empty rhetoric.

Winning American politicians over to a strategy of peaceful engagement was not easy. The essence of the cold war, after all, was conflict, not cooperation. Eastern-European émigrés poured opprobrium on Zbig because they regarded all cooperation with communist governments as treason. Brzezinski stubbornly argued that peaceful engagement could set in action forces that would lead to the erosion of the iron curtain; forgoing contact and rejecting the idea of the slightest compromise, on the other hand, was a way of making the status quo permanent. Thus there was a sensible alternative to the overt armed conflict that would mean mutual destruction.

The cover of *Newsweek* on November 25, 1963, featured a giant portrait of Mao and the question: "Red China: A Paper Dragon?" Inside, seventeen of the magazine's reporters told about what was going on in China and asked, "Can the U.S. exploit the Sino-Soviet rift? . . . For one deeply knowledgeable view, *Newsweek* turned to Prof. Zbigniew Brzezinski, director of Columbia University's Research Institute on Communist Affairs." The title of Zbig's article was "Calculations and Suggestions."

> *China is simultaneously in the midst of three revolutions: a nationalist, an industrial, and a Communist. This unprecedented combination creates intense feelings of enthusiasm and animosity that are likely to dominate the Chinese international outlook for some time.*
>
> *As long as the Sino-Soviet dispute was primarily strategic and ideological it was always possible that some reconciliation was possible. But the escalation of the dispute into a bitter territorial hostility, reawakening deep-rooted historical conflicts, makes a real reconciliation unlikely.*
>
> *American-Soviet conflicts are still more dangerous and more fundamental than American-Chinese differences, with China still basically only a regional power.*

*Although today China is directing its main hostility at the United States, its basic national-territorial interests are more directly in conflict with those of the Soviet Union, than with America.*

Bearing that in mind, writes Brzezinski, the US policy towards China should:

*Strive to disapprove the Chinese calculation that a sustained commitment to national liberation struggles and local wars will force the „imperialist" powers to yield gradually. Anything less than resolute refutation of this Chinese thesis actually would weaken the Soviet conviction that local conflicts are risky and would incline also the Soviets into similar ventures;*
*Continue the policy of isolating China, since this inevitably feeds back into the Sino-Soviet relationship and intensifies Chinese hostility to the Russian's policy of coexistence with the United States. In the longer range, if the Chinese do not moderate, it is likely that Japan will increasingly emerge as a political force in Asia. If, however, the internal evolution of Chinese regime, especially after Mao's death, should involve greater moderation, then it might be in the American interest to adjust our policy accordingly. A weak China is in Russia's interest; Russia can continue pressing the West without fear of its rear. A stronger China might press the Soviet Union into a better relationship with the West.*

And the ultimate conclusion:

*America is blessed with two friendly and much weaker neighbors. Russia is seeing the emergence both in the east and in the west of major powers, and both of them have more than*

> *hinted at the desirability of partitioning the Soviet Union. In those circumstances, American goodwill and restraint will become more and more vital to the Soviets' national interest. This gives us the opportunity of deflecting the Chinese threat regionally while gaining an impressive lever against the Soviet Union if it misbehaves globally.*

This is only part of what Brzezinski wrote in *Newsweek*—the better part of half a century ago. It's not Agatha Christie and it's not light, easy, or pleasant reading. It might even seem just as surprising that a popular news magazine would carry such an extensive and challenging text by a young academic as that his prescriptions lost so little of their currency. Fifteen years later, in the White House, Brzezinski would put them into practice.

The following week's issue covered the murder of President Kennedy in Dallas. His death came as a personal blow to Brzezinski. However, Zbig was to work much more closely with Kennedy's successor, Lyndon Baines Johnson. The Head of the Policy Planning Council at the State Department convinced him to take two years off from academia in order to reinforce the strategic group that suggested foreign policy initiatives to the president.

Zbig's ideas found their way quickly into speeches by a president who met with Brzezinski at the White House more often than is customary.

On November 14, 1966, *Newsweek* ran an article titled "The Thinker," devoted to Brzezinski and including a picture of him captioned "A rising star."

> *When his name appears on a Washington guest list, it looks like typographical error, and few maitre d's along M Street have bothered to learn how to pronounce it. Yet Zbigniew Brzezinski, a brilliant 38-year-old political scientist, is one of the fastest-rising stars in the Johnson Administration. Appointed*

> *four months ago as a braintruster on the State Department's Policy Planning Council, he has already become one of the architects of U.S. foreign policy. "Institutionally," remarks an astute observer of the Great Society pecking order, "his position is not an important one. But everyone is now aware that Brzezinski has the ear of those in power—and that means he's a power, too.". . . . when President Johnson turned his attention toward improving U.S.-Soviet relations, Policy Planning chief Henry Owen tapped Brzezinski as the logical choice to help formulate the policy. From his modest, one-room office on the seventh floor of the State Department, Brzezinski has churned out an endless flow of ideas. And many of these— enthusiastically promoted by Owen and Presidential assistant Walt Rostow—have already surfaced in public.*

Newsweek goes on to describe Zbig as

> *the kind of hard-nosed intellectual who does not suffer fools gladly. Once, asked if he had read a speech by President Kennedy, he shot back: Yes, I helped work on it." And when he discusses his hawkish position on Vietnam, he is apt to act as though he had a monopoly on the truth. Yet even those whom he sometimes rubs the wrong way readily admit that Brzezinski is a veritable dynamo of fresh ideas. Says one top White House aide: "I'd rather talk for a half hour with Brzezinski than with anybody else in Washington." . . . This enthusiasm for Brzezinski's intellect apparently extends all the way to President Johnson.*

Several months earlier, on August 8, 1966, a Newsweek cover titled "Mao and China" showed the Great Helmsman carrying on a tray busts of three rivals, Deng, Liu-Shao Tsi, and Marshall Lin Piao. Inside was an article about the president's national security adviser, Walt Rostow. What does it tell us about Rostow? First, that the president calls him several times a day. Second, that he steers America's destiny abroad. Third, that he is an eternal optimist. And fourth, that he "brought the excellent Brzezinski to the State Department."

President Johnson accepted with regret Zbig's decision to return to the university, but such was the agreement between them.

In 1971, Brzezinski spent half a year in Japan. He traveled there as a Ford Foundation fellow to analyze the role the country could play in the international arena. On returning, he wrote *The Fragile Blossom*, an attempt at answering the question of how Japan was changing and what the changes meant inside and outside the country. He added a caveat that the book was a mixture of analysis and speculation, because he did not regard himself as a specialist on the subject.

In view of its vast dependence on imported raw materials and the lack of its own military potential, Brzezinski pronounced, Japan is like a delicate flower: lovely, but sensitive. The insufficient understanding of Japan in America and the lack of attention to the country trouble him. He recommends fostering Japanese realism rather than encouraging the country's belief in its exceptionality or the special role it should play in Asia. He advises prompting Tokyo to play a greater role in international peacekeeping missions, for instance in the Middle East, where Japan has important economic interests. He warns against inciting rivalry between Japan and China, favoring trilateral Japanese-American-Chinese consultation instead. Finally, he recommends regular annual meetings of the leaders of Japan, Western Europe, and the United States. At the same time, he advocates informal dialogue among social elites, such as the Monet Action Committee and the Bilderberg Group—founded in 1954 by a Pole, Jozef Retinger (who was its chairman for many years), a friend in his youth of Joseph Conrad and later an acquaintance of Clemenceau and Churchill. A longtime member of the Bilderberg Group—

regarded by conspiracy theorists as a nefarious plot, consortium of revisionists, or world government—was David Rockefeller, heir to a legendary fortune and head of New York's great Chase Manhattan Bank.

Rockefeller was thinking along the same lines as Brzezinski. He recalls becoming aware in the early seventies of the dramatic changes in the global balance of power. While the United States remained unrivaled, Western Europe and Japan had picked themselves up out of the rubble and were entering a period of rapid growth, reducing America's proportional share. In the course of international meetings of the his bank's executives in London, Brussels, Montreal, and Paris, Rockefeller brought up the idea of creating an "international peace and prosperity commission" to bring private individuals from the NATO countries and Japan together to discuss such issues as trade and investment, the natural environment, crime control, and aid to the poorest nations.

> *I thought it essential to include the Japanese for a number of reasons—remarks Rockefeller in his Memoirs. First of all, Japan had become a global economic power, and its high-quality products, especially automobiles and electronics, had made inroads into markets everywhere. Japanese export success, however, had produced a hostile reaction in the United States and Europe, and there was a strong perception that Japan was a "free rider" on the international trading system, aggressively exploiting opportunities abroad while only grudgingly opening their domestic market. Japan's economic prowess combined with its curious reluctance to engage seriously in international dialogue made it imperative to include them in the process I had in mind.*
>
> *Zbigniew Brzezinski, then teaching at Columbia University, was a Bilderberg guest that year, and we spoke about the idea on the flight to Belgium that year. I had been urging the*

> *Steering Committee to invite Japanese participants for several years, and at our session that April, I was politely but firmly told no. Zbig considered this rebuff further proof that my idea was well founded and urged me to pursue it."*

Rockefeller organized further meetings with Brzezinski and his colleagues from Harvard, the Brookings Institution, and the Ford Foundation, and they all supported the idea of a three-cornered organization. They followed up by inviting several Japanese, among them future foreign minister Saburo Okita and future prime minister Kiichi Miyazawa. Brzezinski agreed to head up the whole enterprise, which was named The Trilateral Commission.

> *We cast our net widely in terms of membership and recruited labor union leaders, corporate CEOs, prominent Democrats and Republicans, as well as distinguished academics, university presidents, and the heads of not-for-profits involved overseas. We assembled what we believed were the best minds in America. The Europeans and Japanese assembled delegations of comparable distinction.*

Among the first invitees to the Trilateral Commission were future Federal Reserve heads Paul Volcker and Alan Greenspan, as well as the little-known governor of the state of Georgia, James Earl Carter.

Rockefeller recalls how Carter promised in his election campaign that his government would include new faces and new ideas if he won. Nevertheless, it was quite a surprise that his team included fifteen members of the Trilateral Commission, including Vice President Walter Mondale, Secretary of State Cyrus Vance, Secretary of Defense Harold Brown, Secretary of the Treasury Michael Blumenthal, and Zbigniew Brzezinski. In his 1975 autobiography *Why Not the Best?* Carter wrote that "membership on the commission has provided me with a splendid learning opportunity, and many of the other members have helped me in the study of foreign affairs." Rockefeller writes that "predictably, I was accused of trying to take control of Carter's foreign policy."

Control of Carter's foreign policy remained in Carter's hands. But its co-creator was his principal mentor from the Trilateral Commission.

## Notes

Rockefeller's idea of bringing Japan into high-level discussions: David Rockefeller. *Memoirs*, pp. 416–417.

"Taking control of Carter's foreign policy": Rockefeller, pp. 417–418.

# PYGMALION REDUX

**"Jimmy who?" asked Newsweek in December 1974 when the little-known provincial politician James Earl Carter threw down the gauntlet to the party bigwigs and joined the battle for the nation's highest office.**

He came across as an amateur who didn't fully understand what he was letting himself in for. People took his appearance among the pretenders for the White House as an unfunny joke. Some regarded it as distasteful—as if an intruder in muddy boots and a wrinkled shirt had crashed an elegant reception. Others reacted with unfeigned, wide-eyed astonishment: Jimmy who?

When Carter announced his candidacy, his term as governor had only a few weeks to run. Skeptics wondered if he wasn't joining the presidential race out of a lack of any other idea of what to do with himself. Others thought that he might be treating the race as a way of prolonging his political shelf life by a year or eighteen months before he took a licking from more serious rivals. Yet Carter was guided neither by terror at the thought of political oblivion nor the prospect of boredom in retirement. He was driven by his inexhaustible energy and the faith that he had a lot to offer.

He made up for his lack of national political experience with intelligence and sharp intuition. He knew how to read public moods, expectations, and longings. Tired out by Vietnam, the country was mired in pessimism and cynicism. Washington scandals had eroded any remaining trust in the institutions of the presidency and Congress. He felt that America was ready for an "outsider," someone untainted by deals and behind-the-scenes manipulation, that the fact that he didn't know Washington and Washington didn't know him would be taken as a plus rather than a minus. His veneer of Southern charm, naiveté, something approaching political virginity and irreproachable ethics masked steely determination and populist talent. It was a particularly good moment for criticizing the privileges of the wealthy, tax loopholes, and three-martini lunches.

With high unemployment and high inflation tormenting the country, voters were interested mostly in the economy and their own wallets. Carter knew, however, that the president of the United States was commander in chief of the most powerful army in the world, that the Soviets were arming themselves to the teeth and making progress, that the Middle East was a powder keg, and that things with an impact on America could happen abroad on any given day. Understanding the outside world was his weak point. Brzezinski came along like a gift from the Providence that Carter always trusted.

They met thanks to the Trilateral Commission. In charge of the organization's work since 1972, Zbig was open to interesting people from diverse places and backgrounds. He was looking for a progressive Democratic governor. Someone mentioned Carter. One of Brzezinski's associates traveled to Georgia to meet him and came back impressed. Carter received an invitation to join the Commission, and accepted it.

Brzezinski and Carter hit it off immediately. They felt empathy, and even a mutual fascination. Zbig's intellect impressed Carter. Brzezinski liked the same things about Carter that would later find resonance among voters: straightforwardness, honesty, and personal courage. At an early stage, Zbig perceived something else in Carter that the majority of Americans never had a chance to see or appreciate, or that didn't particularly mean anything to them: undeniable intelligence, openness to new ideas, curiosity about the world, and a hunger for information. Finally, his new pupil's sensitivity to social injustice won Zbig's respect.

Brzezinski was not put off by the fact that Carter was born again or that he always kept his religion front and center, because he did not doubt the authenticity of the candidate's faith. He felt that this was Carter's moral compass, and regarded it as preferable to the way other occupants of the White House had turned to alcohol. Brzezinski saw Carter's potential. After Carter's eloquent and impassioned speech on the Middle East situation made a big impression on him at a Trilateral Commission meeting in 1975, Brzezinski shared his impressions with his wife, Muszka. She encouraged him to bet on a horse he liked.

Carter was like a sponge: he soaked up knowledge. Brzezinski not only taught him and polished him like an uncut diamond. Importantly, he also made him credible in the eyes of the elite.

"Those Trilateral Commission meetings for me were like classes in foreign policy—reading papers produced on every conceivable subject, hearing experienced leaders debate international issues and problems, and meeting the big names like Cy Vance, Harold Brown and Zbig," Hamilton Jordan quotes Carter as saying.

Jordan goes on to explain that

> Governor Jimmy Carter admired the experienced Vance, who moved so easily and gracefully through the corridors of power. And while Cy Vance became his acquaintance, Zbig Brzezinski became his friend. At first, Brzezinski was amused by the little-known Georgia governor and his insatiable curiosity about foreign policy, and regularly sent him articles and books to read and later looked over his speeches on foreign policy. "Zbig became my teacher," Carter recalled. As the Carter candidacy progressed, demanding more thoughtful positions

*and public statements on foreign policy, it was only natural for Jimmy Carter to tell his staff, "Check this with Zbig."*

Even when Carter began gaining popularity and winning primaries, the party aristocracy and the labor unions, the traditional pillar of Democratic support, both felt uneasy with him. He was just too different. But he learned with astonishing alacrity. He gathered outstanding figures around himself. He made Lawrence Klein, a University of Pennsylvania professor who would win the 1980 Nobel prize, the head of his economic advisors. His main foreign policy advisor, of course, was Brzezinski.

After the election came a fierce battle for Carter's soul. At least that is how Averell Harriman saw it. Son of a railroad baron and the founder of an investment bank back in the twenties, Harriman accompanied Churchill to his 1942 meeting with Stalin in Moscow, was at Roosevelt's side in Teheran and Yalta, and served as ambassador to Moscow from 1943-1946, secretary of commerce in Truman's cabinet, and governor of New York from 1955-1958. He was a legend of the Democratic Party, which he joined (switching allegiance after previously being a Republican) in 1928. It never crossed Harriman's mind that Carter could become president. When a journalist asked him about the former Georgia governor's chances, Harriman snorted, "What an idea—I've never even met him." Once the former peanut farmer won the White House as a Democrat, however, it was Harriman who had a historical obligation to make sure it didn't all go wrong. Thus he should have a say in filling the key roles. In such an important question as relations with Moscow, who was best suited to showing the greenhorn who, where, why, and how? Anyone but that aggressive Pole, so cocksure and ready to jump at the Kremlin's throat. Much earlier, during the Johnson presidency, Harriman and Brzezinski had been embroiled in a spat involving, among other things, American-Soviet relations. Harriman stated publicly that Brzezinski was above all a Pole who wanted confrontation between Washington and Moscow, and that President Johnson should be aware of this "deformity." The criticism stung Zbig all the more because it came from the man Spiro Agnew, Nixon's unfortunate vice president, had once accused of selling Poland for "two race horses" received as a present from Stalin. As a man of action, Harriman had no intention of accepting the fact that Brzezinski might tinker with American foreign policy.

Richard Holbrooke, then 35, was foreign policy coordinator in Carter's transition team and therefore had the role of introducing Carter to Harriman. Harriman established contact between the president-elect and the Kremlin, bypassing Brzezinski. Harriman visited Brezhnev and presented him with a letter from the new, still-not-completely-assembled administration. Moscow also had an interest in creating an informal back channel with the fledgling future president, and Soviet Ambassador Dobrynin made an unusual gesture by flying to Harriman's residence in Florida to deliver Brezhnev's reply personally. Harriman summoned Holbrooke, and the two of them drafted a response from Carter to Brezhnev before flying to Georgia for consultation with the president-elect. This whole chain of events took place without Zbig's knowledge. There was a whispering campaign underway against Brzezinski, featuring all his real and imagined defects. Once again, Harriman questioned his "Americanism." This was one thing that Brzezinski found out about, and he reacted sharply. He wrote a letter of protest to Harriman, labeled the whispering campaign undignified, and bit back by mentioning baldly that he had not yet said anything to anyone about the traditionally close relations between Harriman and Stalin (and all of Stalin's successors in the Kremlin) or about Harriman's dacha in Crimea.

When Carter phoned Holbrooke in the closing days of November for consultations on appointees, Holbrooke named his favorites but mentioned neither Brzezinski nor the post of national security advisor. When Carter asked him straight out, Holbrooke wriggled.

He did not dare to be completely sincere, so he hedged: Brzezinski was truly able and deserving, but there were doubts about how well he would work together with the secretary of state—Vance was already a dead certainty for this post. Carter icily thanked Holbrooke for his advice.

On December 15, Carter phoned Brzezinski to ask him a favor: Would Zbig serve as his national security advisor? He added that he had made the decision himself, long before. He had taken the time to consult with others about it. On his first day in office he sent a circular letter to the entire White House staff: Do you know how to spell and pronounce "Zbigniew Brzezinski"?

In *Keeping Faith: Memoirs of a President*, published in 1982, Jimmy Carter writes:

> Zbigniew Brzezinski was perhaps the most controversial member of my team. I first met him in 1973, when we were both participants in various conferences on foreign affairs. [he did not add that Brzezinski had invited him to these conferences—A.L.]. Zbig was astute in his analyses, particularly knowledgeable about broad historical trends affecting the industrialized nations and a firm believer in a strong defense for our country and in the enhancement of freedom and democratic principles both here and abroad. His proposals were innovative and often provocative, and I agreed with the—most of the time. Originally from Poland, he had made a special study of the Soviet Union and Eastern Europe. He was interested in China, the Middle East, and Africa; so was I. I was an eager student, and took advantage of what Brzezinski had to offer. As a college professor and author, he was able to express complicated ideas simply. We got to know each other well.
>
> As a volunteer, Zbig helped me during the presidential campaign. I would study his position papers on foreign affairs

*in order to develop my answers to those questions all candidates had to face. He became a frequent visitor to Plains and went out to San Francisco to brief me for my second television debate with President Ford, which was devoted to defense and foreign affairs.*

*He received high recommendations from many sources, but a few of the people who knew him well cautioned me that Zbig was aggressive and ambitious, and that on controversial subjects he might be inclined to speak out too forcefully. When I was making my final decisions about my White House staff and considering him as National Security Advisor, an additional note of caution was expressed: Dr. Brzezinski might not be adequately deferential to a secretary of state.*

*Knowing Zbig, I realized that some of these assessments were accurate, but they were in accord with what I wanted: the final decisions on basic foreign policy would be made by me in the Oval Office, and not in the State Department. I listened carefully to all the comments about him, and decided that I wanted him with me in the White House. (In looking at my old notes, I find interesting that Vance recommended Brzezinski for this job, and Zbig recommended Cy for Secretary of State. Both were good suggestions.)*

When Carter made his final decision, Harriman undertook a conciliatory gesture toward Zbig. He offered him an apartment in his splendid estate in the heart of Georgetown for use until the Brzezinskis found the right house for themselves. Zbig took up the offer and lived at the Harrimans' for half a year.

On February 19, 1977, a month after the inauguration, Brzezinski suggested to the president that each Saturday he would send him, as "part of his weekend reading," a concise report on national security issues. It would contain both facts and Brzezinski's opinions. Carter replied "I like it," and that was the beginning of Brzezinski's weekly correspondence with the president. The title of each memorandum was NSC Weekly Report. Brzezinski wrote 162 of them. They not only review what was happening and what Brzezinski thought of events, but also offer insights into Carter's way of thinking and relations with Zbig. Carter read some of them without comment, but he often added questions, assessments, or marginal remarks like "that's interesting" or "very good," yet he refrained from arguing with Brzezinski or criticizing his judgment.

NSC Weekly Report # 48, February 24, 1978

*a President must not only be loved and respected; he must also be feared. . . . I suspect that an impression has developed that the Administration (and you personally) operates very cerebrally, quite unemotionally. In most instances this is an advantage; however, occasionally emotion and even a touch of irrationality can be an asset. Those who wish to take advantage of us ought to fear that, at some point, we might act unpredictably, in anger, and decisively. If they do not feel this way, they will calculate that simply pressing, probing, or delaying will serve their ends. I see this quite clearly in Begin's behavior, and I suspect that Brezhnev is beginning to act similarly.*

*This is why I think the time may be right for you to pick some controversial subject on which you will deliberately choose to act with a degree of anger and even roughness, designed to have a shock effect. Obviously, the timing and the object ought to be calculated very deliberately, and Congressional support should be mobilized.*

*The central point is to demonstrate clearly that at some point obstructing the United States means picking a fight with the (to be continued once ZB sends a copy)*

Brzezinski told me that Carter did not like the report, even though he wrote nothing in the margins indicating this.

On numerous occasions, the president rejected courses of action that smacked of manipulation. In Report No. 55 of April 21, 1978, for example, Brzezinski wrote about the arcana of diplomacy and mentioned that a demonstration of strength is sometimes necessary to enhance credibility, and that it is sometimes necessary to say one thing in public and something entirely different in confidential negotiations. In the margins, Carter wrote: "You want me to lie?" When Brzezinski suggested preparing several "black propaganda" operations, Carter's response was: "Zbig, you would be wasting your time."

Carter knew that Zbig would lend intellectual support not only to him, but also to other important actors on the political scene. In a diary entry dated November 30, 1977, the president records:

> *I had lunch with Secretary Brown, the Joint Chiefs of Staff, and Brzezinski. I wanted to know if they feel adequately involved in the decisions being made about defense and to a secondary degree about politics. They wanted Brzezinski to come and give them and the CINCS (the commanders in chief) a strategic briefing on the worldwide situation and then (repeat this) monthly. It is important for me to have them on my side on difficult political matters and also helpful to have a military input into some of the questions that we have to decide concerning Okinawa, Panama, Cyprus, sales of military weapons, NATO, plus of course the obvious matters of SALT and comprehensive test ban. It was a very good and constructive meeting.*

The subject of tense relations between the national security council and the state department recurs in the president's memoirs. Carter mentions that Brzezinski had a relatively small staff of top-level experts who were not hindered by the inertia of bureaucratic machinery or by marking time until they retired. The same could not be said of the state department, which by its very nature is above all cautious and restrained. Carter expected that part of the secretary of state's role would be explaining to the American people why the administration had chosen one position rather than another. This required contact with the press and readiness to appear on TV programs or deliver addresses on university campuses. Vance was uncomfortable in such a role; Brzezinski reveled in it. In a natural way, Carter writes, Zbig captured the public's attention.

> *During all the difficult times we faced, I never knew Zbig to try to avoid criticism by shifting blame to his boss. . . . To me, Zbigniew Brzezinski was interesting. He would probe constantly for new ways to accomplish a goal, sometimes wanting to pursue a path that might be ill-advised—but always thinking. We had many arguments about history, politics, international events, and foreign policy—often disagreeing strongly and fundamentally—but we still got along well."*

On May 2, 1980, a few months after Vance's resignation, Carter reflected that

> *Among all my cabinet officers, Cy Vance was philosophically closest to me, but his first loyalty was to the State Department bureaucracy. He always finessed my suggestions that I come over there and have a direct session with his subordinates, and he threatened to resign on numerous occasions when he felt that Harold Brown, Bob Strauss, Sol Linowitz, Zbig Brzezinski, Warren Christopher, or anyone else might be given too significant a part to play in foreign affairs. It was almost impossible for me to get an innovative idea from State,*

*and its primary role seemed to be to put brakes on any proposal that originated elsewhere.*

Carter gradually came around to Brzezinski's view of international events, and especially his sensitivity to Moscow's aggressive policies. In his diary entry for March 13, 1980, Carter writes about a meeting with Franz Josef Strauss, leader of the CSU (the Christian Social Union of Bavaria, the political party). Strauss told Carter about his discussions with the French on the subject of the Soviet invasion of Afghanistan. To their assertion that the invasion was sign of weakness rather than strength, Carter reports, Strauss replied, "'How many expressions of weakness will be necessary before Soviet troops are in Paris?' I liked him, but I can understand why in the campaign he let [Helmut] Kohl, the president of their party, be the public spokesman, while he takes a more moderate posture as a candidate. He could frighten people."

In the context of intelligence reports about Soviet preparations to invade Poland, Carter noted in his diary under the date December 11, 1980: "Zbig expressed his concern, which I share, about the Finlandization of Germany, where they're an ally but everything is decided on whether it will or will not displease the Soviets."

There was room in their relationship for jokes and affection. Brzezinski writes in his memoirs about the frequent meetings with Dobrynin. There was a photograph showing Dobrynin and Brzezinski drinking vodka in the latter's White House office. Carter obtained a print of the snapshot and sent it to his advisor with a note reading: "Now I see why we always get out-traded by the Soviets."

When the president sent Brzezinski off unexpectedly on an emergency trip when Brzezinski had scheduled his son's confirmation, Carter offered to stand in. "Next to members of my family, Zbig would be my favorite seatmate on a long-distance trip," wrote Carter. "We might argue, but I would never be bored."

# ANDRZEJ LUBOWSKI

— ★ —

# Notes

The impact of Trilateral Commission meetings on Carter: Hamilton Jordan, *Crisis: The last year of the Carter Presidency*, p. 45.

"Governor Jimmy Carter admired the experienced Vance . . . " Jordan, p.46.

"Zbigniew Brzezinski was perhaps the most controversial member of my team. . . ": Carter, *Keeping Faith: Memoirs of a President*, pp. 51–52.

"During all the difficult times we faced . . . " : *Keeping Faith*, p. 54.

"Among all my cabinet officers . . . ": Carter, *White House Diary*, p. 425.

Carter on Franz Josef Strauss: *White House Diary*, p. 410.

"Never bored" with Brzezinski: *Keeping Faith*, p. 54.

# A PIANO PIECE
# FOR FOUR HANDS

---

"Young man, I don't care what the facts are. The perception is that there are two voices in foreign policy—and that is hurting the President! There can only be one spokesman in foreign policy—and that spokesman has to be the Secretary of State. The NSC Advisor should be a first-class clerk, but he cannot be a public spokesman. The National Security Advisor should be like a child at a formal dinner—seen but not heard." With these words, Averell Harriman barged into the office of President Carter's chief of staff, Hamilton Jordan.

"I listened but respectfully disagreed, saying that the stories about Vance and Brzezinski were greatly exaggerated. And they were," writes Jordan.

"Except that the difference between a great exaggeration and only a slight exaggeration are matters of definition and open to discussion.

In recent United States history, the center for making the most important decisions in foreign policy has shifted from the State Department to the White House. The president's national security advisor, supported by a relatively small staff, has gradually gained the upper hand over the great apparatus of diplomacy concentrated in the State Department. For purely logistical reasons alone, the national security advisor, chosen by the president with no need for congressional confirmation and sitting behind a desk in the White House, has easier and more frequent access to the president than the senate-confirmed secretary of state. Relations between these two key presidential advisors vary in accordance with their personalities, ambitions, and, above all, the preferences of the president himself. At times, the national security advisor remains in the shadows, avoiding the cameras and microphones. At other times, he steps into the limelight.

If Brzezinski is universally regarded as one of the most controversial national security advisors to any president, it is less because of the policies he favored or the advice he proffered than the conflicts, real or putative, that existed between him and Secretary of State Cyrus Vance—and even more so, because of the noisy, public feuding between his staff and the officials in the State Department. Anatoly Dobrynin, the Soviet ambassador in Washington for 24 years—he took up his post just before the outbreak of the Cuban crisis in 1962, and outlasted seven American secretaries of state—stated that the Carter presidency supplied more controversies and heated debates between leading administration figures than any other president's term of office.

The question is whether this was how it really was and if so, why? What was the nature of the conflict, and what consequences did it have for the presidency of Jimmy Carter?

How was it seen by outside observers, by insiders, and, finally, by the "accused" himself?

Brzezinski comes in for acerbic criticism in Ivo H. Daalder and I. M. Destler's *In the Shadow of the Oval Office*, devoted to presidential national security advisors from the administrations of John F. Kennedy to George W. Bush. The authors cite Brent Scowcroft, national security advisor to Gerald Ford and George H. W. Bush, who held that the advisor has two roles to play: as coordinator and broker in the process of decision-making and implementation, and as the president's main counselor. In his opinion, Brzezinski concentrated on the second of these roles while neglecting the first. What mattered most to him was hardcore politics, rather than the process of making decisions while taking all the options under consideration.

In a conversation with me, Jim Hoagland, the veteran *Washington Post* reporter, looked back on those days:

> *I returned to the US in 1977, as the new Administration was moving in. From 1977 until 1979 I was covering the State Department for the paper, so I was there often, meeting with officials at all levels. Rivalries and animosities are the daily staple of Washington. George Schultz-Caspar Weinberger—The State and the Pentagon—was a good example. But all that pales in comparison with the animosities between Brzezinski and Vance animosities, or to be more precise, animosities between the staffs at the NSC and State. The two men always claimed to have good relations, and it may well be true. They certainly made strong efforts to avoid appearance of personal conflict. But their staffs very frequently clashed, and when that happened, neither Brzezinski nor Vance did much to rein them in.*

Hamilton Jordan recalls that, when the president formally included him in the foreign policy process in January 1978, he was amazed how often Brzezinski and Vance were in agreement—with the sole, important exception of US-USSR relations. "Cy Vance was solid as a rock and completely predictable. He went to the State Department with a clear idea of what he wanted to accomplish," Jordan notes. "While admiring some of Kissinger's achievements, Vance felt that there was a better way for the United States to do business. No diplomatic hocus-pocus, shuttles, or sleight-of-hand were needed to pursue America's interests. Just hard work and a steady course would get the job done."

It would be hard to find a more perfect opposite to Vance than Kissinger, who put his own image above everything else. When Vance met with the media, and these were rare encounters, "he was America's foreign policy accountant, methodically ticking off our positions, decisions, and option. Vance didn't have an ounce of the self-promoter in him" writes Jordan in his memoir *Crisis: The Last Year of the Carter Presidency*. "And if Cy Vance didn't have an ounce of the self-promoter in him, then Zbig had several pounds," adds Jordan. "Encouraged by the President, the proud Pole moved quietly into the vacuum that Vance left for explaining and defending the Administration's foreign policy."

Although both Brzezinski and Vance favored arms reduction and the SALT II agreement, they differed sharply over questions of policy towards Moscow, and especially the proportion between cooperation and rivalry. Brzezinski saw relations with the Kremlin above all as an arena for competition, whereas Vance was significantly more conciliatory.

Since Carter set great stock in personal diplomacy, shortly after the inauguration Brzezinski suggested that the President initiate private correspondence with top world leaders. "I did not see these letters as a substitute for negotiation—he wrote in his memoirs—nor was I naïve enough to think that they would, in and of themselves, resolve any outstanding issues. Nonetheless, I felt that they could be a useful mechanism for developing a personal relationship with key foreign leaders. The first letter to Brezhnev was sent on January 26. It was preceded by some drafting negotiations between Vance and me, which foreshadowed later differences." The letter was generally friendly in tone and Brezhnev's response had been relatively positive. Carter decided to follow up with a much broader agenda. He directed Vance and Brzezinski to develop a response which, according to his handwritten note would be "personal and specific, including in particular comments on SALT II (less cruise missiles and Backfire?),

SALT III (substantial reductions), demilitarized Indian Ocean, prior notice of all missile test firings, throw-weight limits, prohibition of mobile missiles (including SS-20), civil defense limitations, reduced arm sales, Berlin, human rights."

"I worried—recalled Brzezinski—this might be too much at once, and suggested that the draft indicate to Brezhnev that any effort to widen our collaboration and to contain our competition must be based on reciprocity. Accordingly, in the message to Brezhnev, the President noted that the US-Soviet "competition—which is real, very expensive, and which neither of us can deny—can at some point become very dangerous, and therefore it should not go unchecked." It also stated that "recently there seems to have been an increasing inclination to create new tensions and constraints in Berlin, which could cause deterioration in the delicate political balance there. I trust that you will help to alleviate these tensions. "The letter also expressed the hope that the Soviet Union would respect all Helsinki accords. To reassure Moscow, carter added that "it is not our intention to interfere in the internal affairs of other nations. We do not wish to create problems for the Soviet Union. But it will necessary for our government to express publicly on occasion the sincere ands deep feelings of myself and our people. Our commitment to the furtherance of human rights will not be pursued stridently or in a manner inconsistent with the achievement of reasonable results. We would, of course, welcome private, confidential exchanges on these delicate areas."

Brezhnev responded in a chilling manner. "I want to talk bluntly about our impression and thoughts it evoked." He ridiculed Carter's concerns regarding Berlin by suggesting that "it is sent to a wrong address." To Carter's comments on human right the Soviet leader's response was that he would not "allow interference in our internal affairs, whatever pseudo-humanitarian slogans are used to present it." He took particular exception to the exchange of letters between President Carter and the Soviet dissident and Nobel Peace

Prize winner, Andrei Sakharov. He described it as "correspondence with a renegade who proclaimed himself an enemy of the Soviet state," and added, "we would not like to have our patience tested in any matters of international policy, including the questions of Soviet-American relations."

Brezhnev's letter was a jolt to Carter, wrote later Brzezinski. "Vance described the letter as "good, hard hitting, to the point." But I read it rather differently. It struck me as being brutal, cynical, sneering, and even patronizing. It certainly was no response to Carter's effort to get a negotiating process going and to establish some measure of even personal correspondence. It was a very sharp rebuff. . . . In some ways I was made to think of the first encounter between Khrushchev and Kennedy when Khrushchev almost tried to talk Kennedy down and tried to browbeat him into concessions. The letter from Brezhnev had a little bit of the same tone."

One of the main accusations against Brzezinski is that he made both his own views and his differences with Vance public. The fact that he appeared in the media considerably more frequently than the secretary of state created the impression that the Carter team was not really a team, but rather a collection of individuals with divergent views. Against a united, tough adversary marching to the beat of a single drummer, this naturally diminished the chances for success. The media gleefully seized on these differences because conflict sells better than harmony. It therefore became current opinion that the president's two main advisors were competing against each other, and that the more impulsive, feisty, and eloquent of them was coming out on top.

Vance was uneasy when Brzezinski, who neither wanted nor intended to conceal his disapproval of Moscow's aggressiveness, resorted openly to the "China card." Reports on Zbig's visit to Beijing included the information that he had challenged his hosts to a race at the Great Wall of China by declaring: "Last one to the top gets to fight the Russians in Ethiopia!" Vance was furious. Despite his denial of the words, the story had already taken on a life of its own. On another occasion Brezinski was more aggressive toward Moscow during a television interview than the head of the State Department wished.

Robert Gates holds that relations between Zbig and Vance were downright hearty. He recalls that the two men regularly played tennis until the moment of Vance's resignation. Brzezinski may well have voiced an opinion that differed from Vance's on occasion, but Gates never heard an ill word from the presidential advisor about the secretary of state. "Brzezinski's struggle with Vance was not personal in the sense of ambition, power, and the perception of influence—their differences were deep, philosophical, and were centered, in the first instance, on how to deal with the Soviet Union," writes Gates. "They agreed on the desirability of SALT, but Vance believed that arms control was so overridingly important that no action should be taken that might jeopardize negotiations or the political relationship necessary for their ultimate success. On one regional dispute after another, Vance saw each as a local conflict and feared that Brzezinski and others would turn it into an East-West issue imperiling his first priority. For Brzezinski, SALT had to be embedded in the overall relationship, a relationship that was potentially cooperative but inherently confrontational—and he was convinced that neither aspect could be managed in isolation from the other."

"As the tempo of world events seemed increasingly to vindicate Brzezinski's pessimistic readings of Soviet intentions, Vance lost more and more battles," wrote *Time* in a commentary on May 12, 1980, when Vance's resignation was announced.

In 1974, while Nixon was still president, Colonel Mengistu Haile Mariam overthrew Haile Selassie, the emperor of Ethiopia. In the face of a secession threat by Eritrea and a Somali-supported insurrection in the desert region, the new government of Ethiopia sought support in Moscow. Choosing which side to support—

Somalia, which was already dependent on the Soviets, or Ethiopia, with ten times the population and access to the strategic oil transport route from the Persian Gulf—was simple enough. The Marxist Mengistu regime signed a military treaty with the Kremlin. Somalia asked Washington for help.

In Gates's opinion, the crisis in Somalia was the first serious conflict between Brzezinski and Cyrus Vance. Brzezinski regarded the encroachment of partisans from Angola into Zaire in March 1977 as testing of the new administration by the Kremlin. He felt that the Soviet intervention in Ethiopia was also a challenge to America by the USSR in the Third World. Vance wanted to treat it in isolation from the rest of Moscow-Washington relations, and in this case his view won out. However, as Gates writes, the United States lost an important ally in Africa (Ethiopia) and countries in the region friendly to America (Saudi Arabia, Sudan, Kenya, and North Yemen) felt threatened. Moscow, in turn, gained a foothold in a geographically and politically important country.

The Soviets were showering Kaddafi with weaponry. In late 1978, aggressive Libyan politics brought the country to the brink of war with Egypt. Kaddafi had his soldiers helping Idi Amin in Uganda and in Chad, and he tried to overthrow the government of Sudan. Gates wrote that

> *After watching from the Ford NSC the Soviet role in the final collapse of Vietnam, their actions in Angola, and their behavior earlier in the 1970s, it seemed apparent to me as I observed from the Carter NSC that the Soviets were continuing to press ahead in the Third World—tactically seizing opportunities, strategically exploiting U.S. unwillingness to become involved again after Vietnam. Whether one agreed with Zbig's proposed actions to raise the costs to the Soviets of this aggressive behavior, his analysis of the consequences—*

*Soviet consolidation of their gains and leaping at the next opportunities—seemed obvious and irrefutable. He understood that Soviet use of Cuban surrogate troops in the Third Word represented a new and different kind of challenge which, if unmet, would inevitably lead to further interventions.*

Gates regarded Vance's hope that diplomatic means could foil the Soviet and Cuban gambits as idealistic and naïve. Vance's position was a sign of weakness and an invitation for further aggressive Soviet moves in the Third World. So it turned out.

Gates felt that bureaucrats in both the State Department and the CIA torpedoed many of Brzezinski's initiatives. He quotes a later assessment by a CIA officer responsible for the USSR (Arnold Horelick), who wrote that "the venture [Memorandum 42—"U.S. Strategy for Non-Military Competition with the Soviet Union"] was doomed from the start and the problem has been how to terminate the exercise with the least damage and visibility, taking into account its originator [Brzezinski]."

Leslie H. Gelb, the assistant secretary of state for political-military affairs, responsible for Soviet-American arms control talks, conventional arms sales, and all matters relating to the use of forces, writes in his book *Power Rules* that "[m]y loyalty to Vance never wavered, but my views fell much closer to Brzezinski's."

*"The main battle of the Carter years was that between the Columbia professor and the Wall Street lawyer. Though Brzezinski outdid Acheson in his passionate anti-Soviet feelings, and Vance went well beyond Kennan's belief in the power of persuasion. Brzezinski and Vance stood even farther apart on most issues than had the two Truman aides. But they did share Carter's commitment to promoting human rights, which became a centerpiece of Carter's foreign policy. It sprang from Vance's conviction that Nixon and Kissinger*

*had strayed too far afield from basic American values, and that their diplomatic maneuvers lacked any semblance of ethical balance."*

In Madeleine Albright's view, Vance and Brzezinski were competing mainly for Carter's heart. Theoretically, the job of the secretary of state is to formulate and implement foreign policy. The job of the national security advisor is to make sure that all elements of national security policy, including defense, diplomacy, and intelligence, are moving in the same direction. His task is to coordinate policy, not to formulate it. In practice, the dividing lines sometimes blur.

Brzezinski felt that the press magnified his differences with Vance because conflict is a better story than harmony. The media incited discrepancies and territorial squabbles between the staffs of the State Department and the National Security office: one of them was on top for a moment, and then the other.

Even before Carter moved into the White House, Vance somewhat awkwardly mentioned to Brzezinski that he would prefer that the latter not receive foreign ambassadors. For practical reasons rather than out of ambition, Brzezinski turned down the idea. Not the best of starts, but after a few months of cooperation Brzezinski described Vance thus in his diary:

*Very well informed, very much to the point, well briefed on most issues, shows a much more factual grasp of international affairs than I ever expected, in many cases better informed than I, quick in responding, quite decisive in tone and in speech, very much interested in negotiating and in procedure. I think he is weaker on the longer-range perspective, overoptimistic on our relations with the Soviets, and does not stand up strongly enough to the President on really important issues. But I really admired his dedication, the long hours* he was putting in, and his readiness to fulfill the Presidential requirements.

In late 1978—after almost two years of working together—he noted that

> It would be difficult to imagine someone better as Secretary of State in terms of personal relationships, even though I am often frustrated by what the Department of State stands for. There is no doubt he is a very good person—extremely loyal, highly dedicated, and willing to do what the President wishes without too much questioning. Moreover, he is really a very decent person. Finally, what is quite impressive is how well briefed he is on most of the issues he has to deal with. He obviously has a lot of energy and a very good memory.

The two men were probably closest when it came to Middle East issues. Begin's unyielding and unimaginative position irritated them both. They both opposed apartheid in South Africa.

As seen in his memoirs, what irritated Brzezinski about both Vance and his successor Warren Christopher was that when, as he puts it, "diplomacy made way for power politics," both of these outstanding diplomats felt more comfortable with endless analyses, questioning proposed courses of action, and bridling at firm decisions.

> He was successful on Wall Street because he was methodical and congenial"—noted Brzezinski—But the contractual-litigational approach which works so successfully in a large law firm was less suited for shaping foreign policy in an age that has become both ideological and revolutionary.... As a member of both the legal profession and the once-dominant Wasp elite, he operated according to their values and rules,

*but those values and rules were of declining relevance not only in terms of domestic American politics but particularly in terms of global conditions.*

Vance, in other words, was a distinguished nice guy who was in over his head. Brzezinski felt that Vance

*would have made an extraordinarily successful Secretary of State in a more tranquil age. There his strongest qualities would have stood up, reinforcing the country's basic decency and commitment to fundamental principle. He was at his best when negotiating with decent parties in the world: the British over Zimbabwe or the Israelis and Egyptians regarding the Middle East peace: he was at his worst in dealing with the thugs of this world. His deep aversion to the use of force was a most significant limitation on his stewardship in an age in which American power was being threatened on a very broad front.*

Brzezinski himself, commenting on the process of foreign policy formulation and its perception, wrote in 1982 that "[t]o a degree, especially in the first year, I tried to use the NSC as the President's "think tank," and I often referred to it as such. . . . Preoccupation with personalities and personal infighting is the logical extension of a lack of interest in history," Brzezinski asserts. "Personalities are more interesting and their coverage intellectually less demanding than the clash of ideas. Hence so much focus on personal and bureaucratic struggles but so little attention to historical and philosophical assumptions on the part of the Washington press corps."

# Notes

Harriman's outburst on the role of national security adviser: H. Jordan, *Crisis. The Last Year of the Carter Presidency,* p.48.

Letter exchange with Brezhnev: Z. Brzezinski. *Power and Principle. Memoirs of the National Security Advisor,* pp. 151–156.

Brzezinski-Vance differences not personal: R. Gates. *From the Shadows,* pp. 71–72.

"After watching from the Ford NSC . . . ": Gates, *From the Shadows,* p. 77.

State Department and CIA torpedoing Brzezinski's initiatives: Gates, p. 76.

"My loyalty to Vance": Leslie H. Gelb, *Power Rules,* p. 59.

"The main battle of the Carter years": Gelb, p. 57.

Brzezinski's positive assessment of Vance as "Very well informed" etc.: *Power and Principle,* p. 37.

"Difficult to imagine someone better as Secretary of State": *Power and Principle,* p. 39.

Op. cit., p. 44.

Brzezinski on the press corps's indifference to history: *Power and Principle,* p. 543.

# ZBIG VS. HENRY

Brzezinski and Kissinger, Kissinger and Brzezinski. Two immigrants—one had to escape from Central Europe and the other could not return to Central Europe. They started on the road to their spectacular careers at the same place, Harvard. Afterwards, they went their separate ways only to end up in the same place again—the most important place in the world, the White House. That is where the similarities end and the differences begin.

One weighs his words as if he were laboriously searching for them among the corners of his memory, and then chews over them with delectation. The other's words rush out as if he were firing them from a machine gun that he loaded beforehand and has been gripping with an itchy trigger finger. One masterfully wraps everything in cotton wool and the other lets fly. Kissinger flirts with the stars on television; Brzezinski tells them that their knowledge about what is going on has revealed itself to be appallingly superficial. The fact of being constantly compared to each other irritates both of them. Neither of them regards the comparison as a compliment.

Brzezinski wanted to change the world and stifle the Kremlin's aspirations because he knew those aspirations were boundless. Kissinger endeavored to patch up the existing order, allocate spheres of influence, and refrain from trying to find up what the other party was up to under the covers.

Where Zbig backed dissidents, Henry avoided them. Zbig earned and never freed himself from a reputation as a hawk, while Henry remained a diplomat in velvet gloves, holding a glass of champagne. Brzezinski posed with a rifle on a mountain pass in Pakistan; Kissinger posed at film premieres with a sex bomb on his arm.

In Kissinger's case it could be sometimes hard to tell what he had just said—whether he was for or against, or both for and against. Brzezinski was always surgically precise, and he always came right out and said things. There were no doubts about what he meant. Sometimes it was worth asking if he should have said it.

They always denied being in competition, but they competed for decades, first at Harvard where there was not enough room for every super-talented individual. Kissinger won out by a nose. He was five years older and earned his doctorate a year later, but managed to outmaneuver his Polish rival. Brzezinski admits that he did have a sense of satisfaction a year and a half later when Harvard offered him full professorship, with half time off free for research for the rest of his life, and he turned it down. He wanted to shape policy and New York offered the better springboard. He landed in New York, closer to the movers and shakers than Boston. If not for Columbia, who knows, if he would have entered into such close cooperation with David Rockefeller. And if not for that cooperation, who can say that the Trilateral Commission, of which Zbig was the *de facto* head for years, would have come into being? If not for the Commission, would he have gotten so close to Carter? And would Carter have had a shot at the presidency without Brzezinski?

As opposed to Henry, Zbig believes that an attachment to values is a source of strength, rather than weakness, in foreign policy. That is why the Republican Ronald Reagan considered the Democrat Brzezinski for a place in his administration. That is why there was no place for Kissinger in the administration of Reagan, who saw the essence of American foreign policy as the fight for freedom rather than the defense of the status quo.

If not for Brzezinski's cocktail of realism and romanticism, there would have been no support for Radio Free Europe, Soviet dissidents, or the Polish Solidarity movement. From his early years Zbig had understood the corrosive influence of communism on a nation's morality. He studied it. He wrote about it. During his first postwar trip to Europe in 1953, he showed up at the Radio Free Europe offices in Munich and declared his willingness to collaborate.

Paraphrasing Goethe, Kissinger once told John Stoessinger, a Harvard colleague: "If I had to choose between justice and disorder, on the one hand, and injustice and order, on the other, I would always choose the latter."

Hans Morgenthau, a leading adherent of the "realist" approach to foreign policy and of differentiating the morality of ordinary people from the morality of statesmen, once said of Kissinger's style that "Henry has a magnificent gift, which I didn't expect of him, having known him for twenty years, to transform himself in every capital into a friend and promoter of the particular country where he happens to be. There is a danger in such diplomacy, which works in the beginning, but doesn't work where the governments have good relations and talk to one another."

Kissinger was aware of this danger, but he could not control his habit. Grappling with the frequent accusations that Kissinger is two-faced, Isaacson quotes leading Israeli politicians like Yitzhak Rabin, who once said that "Kissinger had a Metternichian system of telling only half the truth. He didn't lie. He would have lost credibility. He didn't tell the whole truth." Shimon Peres observed to Rabin that "with due respect to Kissinger, he is the most devious man I've ever met."

One of the Nixon archive tapes released in 2011 reveals Henry telling the president, after the two men heard Israeli Prime Minister

Golda Meir appeal for aid to Soviet Jewry during a meeting in 1973, that "the emigration of Jews from the Soviet Union is not an objective of American foreign policy. And if they put Jews into gas chambers in the Soviet Union, it is not an American concern. Maybe a humanitarian concern."

During the 1968 presidential campaign, Kissinger's patron Nelson Rockefeller spent a long time making up his mind about whether to run. Someone asked Kissinger how much time he would be able to devote to the campaign if Rockefeller took the plunge. Joseph Persico, then a speechwriter for the New York governor, recalls, according to Isaacson, that Kissinger replied: "not as much as Nelson will want." If that was the case, Persico suggested, then perhaps Brzeziński should be Rockefeller's adviser. "Not at all the required depth," Kissinger shot back. Persico had the impression that Kissinger consulted his calendar and concluded in an instant that he would be able to put more time into the campaign after all.

The story that Kissinger offered his services to both Republicans and Democrats in 1968, even sharing the opposition research material known as the "shit files," that the Rockefeller campaign staff had collected against Nixon, was published in 1983 by Seymour M. Hersh.

During the George H. W. Bush presidency, Kissinger came up with an idea that James Baker christened "Yalta II." In broad terms it envisioned a secret pact with the Kremlin: Moscow would consent to liberalization in Eastern Europe in exchange for a promise from America not to exploit the situation against the Soviets. In January 1989, Kissinger shared the idea with Gorbachev, who regarded it as unrealistic because the USRR was already struggling to stay on its feet; but in view of who was proposing it he looked for some catch and wondered what the hidden intentions were. A Soviet expert in the State Department summed it all up concisely: "Why buy what history is giving you for free?" When the idea leaked, Brzezinski published an article in The *New York Times* with a barbed reference to Kissinger: "Others even advocate, in the tradition of realpolitik, an American-Soviet deal regarding Eastern Europe, a kind of new Yalta."

The media could not resist the temptation of drawing analogies between Kissinger and Brzezinski as two professors with foreign accents summoned to Washington one after the other to shape "global strategy."

Hamilton Jordan regarded the analogy as unfounded. For him, the proof lay in the two men's relations with subordinates and the media. Jordan notes that White House staffers regarded Kissinger, the darling and star of the media, as a mercurial egomaniac who worked people to death. Most of his staff admired his intelligence and some respected him, but very few of them liked him. Things were far different with Zbig. On the outside, he was regarded as obsessive. He was less deft than Kissinger at self-deprecating humor. His stern intelligence reinforced the hard-line image and this made many people uncomfortable. Those who worked with him or knew him better, however, often fell under his charm. He demanded much from his subordinates but they liked him, and Zbig created a team spirit in the National Security Council that had been absent in Kissinger's time.

"I found a playful, almost childlike quality about Zbig that contrasted sharply with his public image. . . . Zbig and I occasionally played tennis on the White House court (we referred to it as 'the Supreme Court'). He was a good athlete and played a hard, intense game—without subtlety. On every shot, he would wind up and knock the hell out of the ball. If the ball made it over the net and dropped inside the lines, it was difficult to return, but his game was so erratic that rallies seldom lasted more than several strokes. Either he smashed a winner, or, more often, he hit into the net or out of bounds. One day I called to him across the net, 'Zbig, you play tennis like you conduct foreign policy.' 'You must mean that every shot is well-planned, crisply hit, low and hard.' 'Yes,' I said, 'and usually out.'"

Madeleine Albright, once Brzezinski's student and later his employee, observes in her memoirs that those who saw him only on television had the impression that he was the harsh character with the sharp edges that editorial cartoonists loved to transform into the figure of a hawk. "I feared him as a professor, but as a boss he was warm. He didn't talk about collegiality but he practiced it. He never introduced us as his staff, but rather as his colleagues."

One White House staffer who saw Kissinger in action said that he fed the press as if they were a flock of birds. "They eat regularly, they eat well, and they sing Henry's song." Brzezinski, on the other hand, was unlucky with the media—and especially with The *Washington Post*, essential reading for those who think they run the country. Having broken the Watergate scandal, the *Post* basked in the glory of vanquishing Nixon. Ben Bradlee, its executive editor, was the ornament of every party worth going to. In December 1979, Sally Quinn, who had recently become Bradlee's third wife, published an article on Zbig in the *Post*. She wrote that Brzezinski had flirted with "a woman reporter" who was interviewing him, that he had suddenly unzipped his fly, and that he had been photographed while doing so. The paper did not print any photographs, but Sally Quinn also gave her readers to understand that the president's adviser picked up sixteen-year-old girls in Washington nightclubs. No one would have been likely to take such a "sensation" to heart if not for the fact that it came out in The *Washington Post*. The astonished Brzezinski and White House press secretary Jody Powell showed the article to Carter. The president was furious. Zbig said that he would take care of it. This was not difficult, because Quinn had never interviewed Brzezinski and there were no photographs. Brzezinski retained a lawyer to explore the possibility of a libel suit. At the *Post*, Ben Bradlee defended the series by Quinn, as a "son of a bitch of a good story." He described the photograph as "very suggestive." The *Post* printed a correction the next day, December 20, 1979:

> *In yesterday's story about Zbigniew Brzezinski, it was stated that at the end of an interview with a reporter from a national magazine—as a joke—Brzezinski committed an offensive act and that a photographer took a picture 'of this unusual expression of playfulness.' Brzezinski did not commit such an act, and there is no picture of him doing so.*

In an article headline "Brzezinski's Zipper Was Up," *Time* wrote:

> *The Iranian crisis was in its seventh week and OPEC was propelling oil prices to historic heights. But in that cosmopolitan capital on the Potomac, the best and the brightest were preoccupied with a more delicate matter: the open or shut case of Zbigniew Brzezinski's fly. As it turned out, President Carter's National Security Adviser had kept his zipper up, and the* Washington Post *was caught with its trousers down.*

A month later, in "Trial by Interview," the same news magazine opined that

> *[o]ne price of being a public figure is to be pursued by a persistent journalist demanding private interviews for a full personality study. Dare the public figure refuse? Zbigniew Brzezinski, the President's National Security Adviser, tried and got the treatment. Sally Quinn's three-part series in the* Washington Post *damaged Brzezinski in passing, but it damaged the* Post *even more. The* Post *is one of the nation's best papers, though nowadays it often seems excessively bent on*

*topping its Watergate success. . . . The* Charlotte Observer *was outraged: "Such errors raise questions about the newspaper's motives as well as its competence."*

Zbig could hardly complain of a shortage of harsh criticism. In a piece titled "Almost Everyone vs. Zbig," Strobe Talbott, *Time* magazine's principal correspondent on Soviet-American relations, later Deputy Secretary of State in the Clinton Administration, and currently the president of the Brookings Institution, wrote:

> *"A man of dazzling intellectual virtuosity and erudition, Brzezinski has sometimes seemed to be badly served by his brilliance. He is so deft at formulating fancy theories, and he so likes to hear himself spin them out, that he has tended to pay less attention than he should to making those theories work in practice—and, indeed, to figuring out whether they can work."* Talbott felt that Brzezinski *"had shown poor judgment in indulging his visceral anti-Russian sentiments. . . . Brzezinski believes that he is under attack because of the politically supercharged atmosphere and because he is vulnerable to both the left and the right: the left resents him, in his view, for being correct about the dangers of Soviet expansionism, while the right criticizes him for supporting the embattled SALT II treaty and the human rights policy."*

Nine years later, Talbott published an interview with Brzezinski titled "Vindication of a Hard-Liner," which begins:
"Q. You've always been a strong critic of the Soviets, yet just in the past month you have been given a standing ovation at the Diplomatic Academy in Moscow, you've been respectfully interviewed in Pravda and even given prime-time coverage on Soviet television. What has it been like for you personally?

"A. Well, I wouldn't be human if I didn't confess to a certain amount of ego gratification. When I stood in front of the foreign policy establishment in the Soviet Union and was given a generally empathetic reception, I had a sense of, if you will, historical vindication."

Robert Gates, the future CIA director and defense secretary who joined Brzezinski's team in May 1977, had a good deal to say about his boss. He recalls in his memoirs that Zbig was organized almost to a fault. He placed high demands on professional analysts. He treated the auxiliary staff with respect and dignity. He had a good sense of humor, but Gates cannot recall his ever making a joke at his own expense. Outsmarting others gave him satisfaction. Admiral Stansfield Turner, the CIA director, pointed out that Brzezinski, rather than Turner, saw the president at 6:30 AM, when the daily schedule called for an intelligence briefing. Turner felt that this was his role. Brzezinski admitted that Turner was right. The next day, Brzezinski showed Turner a schedule on which the president's 6:30 AM appointment featured as the "national security briefing."

"He debated like he played tennis," recalls Gates, "to win and to win all the time. The intellectually weak or deficient or slow merited no sympathy. Sometimes, his combative instincts overcame his good judgments and he would reject ideas or approaches simply in the course of winning a debater's point. Accordingly, whenever I had a controversial problem or issue to raise with him, I would do it in writing. I advised others to do likewise. His reactions to the written word were always more considered, more reflective, and better balanced. Then, and now, I considered him by far the most realistic, experienced, and balanced of Carter's foreign policy team. He was also a pleasure to work for."

Gates remembers accompanying Zbig on a trip to Cairo. After concluding his talks with Sadat, Brzezinski had some free time. They decided to take in the pyramids and the Sphinx, but an ABC

TV crew caught up with them there. Out of a desire to preserve his boss's privacy, Gates kept obstructing the cameraman. "When we returned home, and he saw the tapes from the news," writes Gates, "he put his hand on my shoulder and told me that I was a bright young man who would undoubtedly go far, but not if I ever again got between him and a TV crew."

Immediately after this, he adds that Brzezinski "wore his ego lighter than most, however, despite all the talk of his wanting to be as significant a figure as Kissinger had been and his supposed rivalry with Kissinger—which, frankly, I never saw."

How has time influenced the way Brzezinski and Kissinger see the world? Zbig was almost obsessively absorbed for decades by the communist threat and the need to respond to Soviet gambits with a firm "no." When that adversary threw in the towel, Brzezinski never for a moment took his eyes off the natural successor, Putin's Russia, which was frustrated, less threatening than the USSR, but still dangerous.

Henry seems to remain unmoved in his conviction about the primacy of order and self-interest over universal humanistic values. In 2011, he published *On China*. Writing about the wave of starvation inflicted by Mao's rule, he gives the number of victims as "more than 20 million," as opposed to the figure twice as high provided by most scholarly sources. He does not mention the destructive scale of the Cultural Revolution, a moral catastrophe that cost China an additional 10 million lives. On the other hand, Kissinger states that "if China remains united and emerges as the superpower of the 21st century," many Chinese may well judge Mao as they judge the earlier emperor Qin Shi, "whose excesses some later acknowledged as a necessary evil."

Discussing the book in the *Financial Times*, Chris Patten, the last British governor of Hong Kong and today the chancellor of Oxford University, asserts that Kissinger's fascination with Mao leads him to skim over the dimensions of the terror and the cruelty of his rule. "My main criticism of Kissinger is not that his commitment to partnership with China is too strong, or that his praise for China's achievements too effusive," Patten writes. "But I wonder whether the tone of his diplomacy is good for China and the rest of us, and whether the way he writes about China betrays a wholly unnecessary tendency, if not to kowtow, then at least to engage in a preemptive deferential bob."

Writing about Kissinger's book in the *New York Times,* Michiko Kakutani observes that: "when it comes to talking about Chinese leaders he has met, Mr. Kissinger, the hardheaded apostle of realpolitik, can sound almost starry-eyed. His sympathy for these leaders is not that surprising given his descriptions of them as practitioners of the same sort of unsentimental power politics he is famous for himself. . . . Mr. Kissinger writes about what he describes as a 'poignant' scene in which 'Nixon complimented Mao on having transformed an ancient civilization, to which Mao replied: "I haven't been able to change it. I've only been able to change a few places in the vicinity of Beijing."' Mr. Kissinger then, startlingly, adds: 'After a lifetime of titanic struggle to uproot Chinese society, there was not a little pathos in Mao's resigned recognition of the pervasiveness of Chinese culture and the Chinese people.' Buying into many of the myths Mao promoted about himself, Mr. Kissinger describes him as 'the philosopher king.'"

What brought about Zbig's metamorphosis? What made the "hawk," who said that the Russians should be taught a lesson and that the longer they bloodied themselves in Afghanistan the better, suddenly begin talking about a global political awakening (an important element in Zbig's 2007 *Second Chance*), dignity, and respecting the Other? This is what my Washington colleagues, the cream of the press corps, urged me to ask about in my next meeting with the subject of this book. I had in fact noted far earlier in Zbig a sensitivity to wrongs and an understanding of the importance of human dignity. That was how I read his support for dissidents and attention to minority rights. Was this solely the result of animosity toward the Soviets? If so—if Zbig wanted to finish the Kremlin off—then why? Was it because he feared that an inebriated general secretary would push the button in Moscow and send the rockets flying toward America? I don't think so. What he really couldn't stand about totalitarianism was the stifling of freedom, the trampling of human dignity, the intolerance for differences of faith or thinking. This was apparent in his master's thesis in Canada more than sixty years ago. Once, he concentrated on a single enemy. Today, when that enemy is gone or when its successor is less potent, he is aware of the awakening of those who had been sleeping, or who had been paralyzed with fear or had not known that things can be different.

In 1994, Kissinger published his 900-page *Diplomacy*. In the index, there is no trace of the name "Brzezinski."

## Notes

"If I had to choose . . . ": Stoessinger, *Henry Kissinger: The Anguish of Power*, p. 14.

Morgenthau, quoted by Isaacson, *Kissinger: A Biography*, p. 555.

Kissinger on Soviet Jewry: *New York Times*, Dec. 10, 2010.

Persico: Isaacson, p. 124.

"Shit files": Hersh, *The Price of Power: Kissinger in the Nixon White House*, p. 14.

Brzezinski's attack on Kissinger: *The New York Times*, March 13, 1989.

Jordan on tennis: *Crisis: The Last Year of the Carter Presidency*, pp. 50–51.

On the *Post* story: *Time*, January 21, 1980.

Talbott's critique: *Time*, September 22, 1980.

Gates's characterization: *From the Shadows: The Ultimate Insider's Story of Five Presidents and How They Won the Cold War*, p.70.

Gates on Brzezinski vs. Kissinger: p. 71.

Patten's review of Kissinger's book: *FT,* May 28/29, 2011.

Kakutani's review: *NYT*, May 9, 2011.

# IF NOT FOR FORD'S GAFFE

---

**Soviet sentries armed with rifles are guarding prisoners in a stone quarry. One of the prisoners, with "Poland" on his back, is leaning toward a neighbor holding a sledge hammer with "Hungary" on his back, and whispering conspiratorially into his ear: "President Ford has announced our independence. Pass it on."**

This editorial cartoon appeared in *Newsweek* on October 18, 1976, immediately after the second televised presidential debate between incumbent President Gerald R. Ford and Jimmy Carter, the Democratic candidate. The jaws of millions of viewers dropped at the moment summed up in the *Newsweek* headline as "Jerry Ford Drops a Brick."

All over America, voters with Eastern European roots reacted with outrage and shock to the president's assertion that "there is no Soviet domination in Eastern Europe," wrote Newsweek. Everybody was saying and writing similar things.

Republican strategists feared that the gaffe would cost Ford votes in six industrial states critical to the election: New York, New Jersey, Pennsylvania, Ohio, Michigan, and Illinois. More than two million people with Eastern European roots lived in these six states.

— ★ —

The so-called "Sonnenfeldt Doctrine" had become a particularly troubling subject for Gerald Ford during the race for the Republican nomination. Helmut Sonnenfeldt was a tall State Department and National Security Council official and a close associate of Henry Kissinger. At a conference in London of 28 American ambassadors accredited in Europe in December 1975, he said something that in the final analysis boiled down to the idea that the acceptance of Soviet domination over the countries of Eastern Europe is the best way to guarantee peace and avoid World War II. A transcript of Sonnenfeldt's remarks was approved by Henry Kissinger and distributed to American ambassadors all over the world as official foreign policy.

The lecture was supposed to be confidential, and when *The New York Times* published it first time, Sonnenfeldt characterized the newspaper's version as slanted, inaccurate, and distorted. The official State Department summary as printed in the NYT on April 5, 1976, is appalling:

"The Soviets' inability to acquire loyalty in Eastern Europe is an unfortunate historical failure because Eastern Europe is within their scope and area of natural interest. It is doubly tragic that in this area of vital interest and crucial importance it has not been possible to establish roots of interest that go beyond sheer power.... With regard to Eastern Europe, it must be in our long-term interest to influence events in this area—because of the present unnatural relationship with the Soviet Union—so that they will not sooner or later explode, causing World War III. This organic, unnatural relationship is a far greater danger to world peace that the conflict between East and West."

Reagan described the "Sonnenfeldt doctrine" as "selling the captive nations down the river and forcing them to accept their own enslavement," and attacked the foundations of the Ford administration's foreign policy. Reagan's main accusation against Kissinger boiled down to the charge that the latter's version of detente was a one-way street. Reagan also denounced Kissinger's treatment of Aleksander Solzhenitsyn, "a genuine moral hero disdained by Kissinger and Ford." Ford managed to win the nomination from Reagan by a narrow margin and went on to face Carter in the general election.

Attacking the president, Jimmy Carter also attacked Kissinger. He spoke of the "Nixon-Kissinger-Ford" foreign policy as "covert, manipulative, and deceptive in style." He also charged that "it runs against the basic principles of this country, because Kissinger is obsessed with power blocs, with spheres of influence." Carter's words were practically a direct quote from Zbigniew Brzezinski.

In *Foreign Affairs* in 1975, Brzezinski wrote that "covert, manipulative and deceptive in style, it seemed committed to a largely static view of the world, based on a traditional balance of power, seeking accommodation among the major powers on the basis of spheres of influence." Many years later Walter Isaacson wrote in his biography of Kissinger that "Hearing Brzezinski's snide words slung at him each day, not with a slightly embittered Polish accent but a smiling Georgia accent, drove Kissinger to near distraction."

The second televised Carter-Ford debate, in San Francisco on October 6, 1976, was dedicated to foreign policy. In one corner—the sitting president, with his experience of negotiations with Brezhnev and meetings with Mao. In the other corner—a farmer who had become governor of a southern state.

The question that unexpectedly tripped up the incumbent concerned the Helsinki Accords that Ford had signed and the unfortunate "Sonnenfeldt Doctrine." It did not require a soothsayer to foresee such a question or questions, and the president's advisers had included a response in their preparation scenario. This response, however, was awkward.

They wanted the president to say that he did not understand all the uproar, and that his visits to Poland, Romania, and Yugoslavia promoted closer American relations with those countries. How, then, could anyone speak about consenting to domination? Ford could also have recalled how, as a congressman, he had flown to the Austrian-Hungarian border in 1956, at the time of the Hungarian Revolution, to greet people fleeing the Red Army, and thus understood the fears and aspirations of the peoples of the region. However, Ford never said this because his advisers did not know that he had been at the Hungarian border in 1956.

When the question about Helsinki was posed during the debate, the president began by noting that not only he and Brezhnev had signed the Accords, but also the heads of more than thirty countries, including the representative of the Holy See. He categorically objected to the interpretation of the Helsinki Accords as consent to Soviet domination of Eastern Europe. If he had stopped there, everything would have been fine. But he plowed on and added that there was no Soviet domination of the region, and would be none as long as he was president. Then he dug deeper. At a certain point, he said: "I don't believe that the Poles consider themselves dominated by the Soviet Union." He named other Central and Eastern European countries that, in his opinion, were not under the Kremlin heel, either.

"I would like to see Mr. Ford convince the Polish-Americans and the Czech-Americans and the Hungarian-Americans in this country," remarked Carter, "that those countries don't live under the domination and supervision of the Soviet Union."

Brent Scowcroft, Ford's national security advisor, went pale. Kissinger, in Washington, watched the debate and phoned an hour later to tell Ford how well he had come across. The media homed in on the president's colossal gaffe. When Scowcroft and White House chief of staff Dick Cheney faced the reporters, the first question was, "Are there any Soviet troops in Poland?" Scowcroft answered yes, there are four divisions there, but the president wanted to say that we do not recognize Soviet domination in Europe. Ford himself was tired and went to bed. The damage had been done. What counted was not what he had wanted to say, but what he had actually said. A week later, he acknowledged that he had expressed himself imprecisely. It was too late. The opponents of detente rounded on the policy and its architect, Kissinger. William Safire wrote in *The Washington Post* that "The verbal gaffe was the President's, but the basic political blunder of Helsinki was the Secretary of State's."

George Gallup, the opinion pollster, called the question, or rather Ford's answer, "the most decisive moment in the campaign."

In the presidential election a month later, Ford polled 1,683,247 fewer popular votes than Carter, a losing margin of 2 percent. However, thanks to the arithmetic of the Electoral College, Ford was much closer than this to victory.

Let's indulge in some fantasizing and sketch out an alternative scenario.

Gerald Ford never committed that fatal gaffe in the televised debate. He does not lose the votes of the flabbergasted and outraged Poles, other Americans of eastern-European origins, and the small numbers of Americans who were put off by the president's ignorance. He does not need much to win. All he has to do is win in Wisconsin, where he lost by 35,245 votes, and Ohio, where Carter's margin was even thinner, at 11,116 votes. Wisconsin is the "most Polish" state in the Union. Almost 60,000 people of Polish origins live in Milwaukee alone. A Polish-American was mayor of Green Bay for a decade and president of the Packers for 24 years. More than 50,000 Poles live in two cities in Ohio, Toledo and Cleveland. Even if Ford's gaffe did not cost him a single vote outside these two states, turning them around would have won him the election. The Wisconsin and Ohio electors would have returned him to the White House by 276 electoral votes to 261.

If Ford had defeated Carter, the world would have been looking forward to four more years of American foreign policy under Kissinger's baton, because Ford had promised publicly that, as long as he was president, Henry would be secretary of state. Kissinger himself had not the slightest inclination to relinquish the privileges of power. His model and hero Metternich was minister for 30 years, and that struck Kissinger, Isaacson notes, as just about right for achieving his goals. Chatting with a friend on board "his" Boeing 707, he once observed: What university would give me a plane like this?

What kind of foreign policy could be expected, in this alternative scenario, from the Ford-Kissinger team? How would it differ from Carter's policies from 1977 to 1981?

Such speculation is risky, of course, but in this case the fact that we are talking about what would have been an unchanged staff reduces the risk. We can assume that the underlying values, inclinations, and temperaments would remain unchanged.

Carter does not proclaim in Annapolis that he is prepared for both cooperation and confrontation with Moscow, which shocked and chilled the Kremlin because no one had used such language before. Kissinger pushes the SALT II disarmament negotiations along. The signing ceremony takes place in the same room in Vienna, but in 1977 rather than 1979. Brezhnev is two years younger, has a better grip on things, and perhaps does not kiss Ford on the lips the way he did Carter. Brezhnev and his foreign minister Andrey Gromyko are spared the sight of that hate-filled Pole who made their blood boil. They might even have forgotten about him. Balance and order—just what the world needs most (in *First Person*, published in 2000, Vladimir Putin recalled a conversation he had with Kissinger in the early 1990s when Kissinger said, according to the book, that he felt Mikhail S. Gorbachev had been too hasty in withdrawing Soviet forces from Eastern Europe). In the late fall of that same year, or the following spring, the United States Senate ratifies SALT II.

Carter writes in his diaries that America's military budget, measured in real dollars, shrank a total of 35 percent in the 8 years preceding his administration, while the Soviet budget was growing at an average of 8 percent annually. In the mid-1970s, America had not yet shaken off the traumas of Vietnam and Watergate, whereas Moscow was steaming ahead in arms procurement. When Americans chose their president in November 1976, the USSR had 1,556 intercontinental ballistic missiles (ICBMs) and the United States 1,054; the Soviets had 799 submarine-launched ballistic missiles (SLBMs) on 60 nuclear-powered subs, as against about 40 such subs on the American side. Soviet vessels patrolled off the American coast. Moscow was arming itself to the teeth and its potential gave it reason to believe in its own might, encouraging international adventurousness. Were Ford and Kissinger ready to stop this trend? No one knows.

In our alternative history we do know, however, that dissidents can kiss any support goodbye. Kissinger's consistency on this issue is well-known; he would not risk upsetting the equilibrium for the sake of Solzhenitsyn, Havel, Michnik, or Solidarity. The fate of Radio Free Europe and Radio Liberty is already hanging by a thread; now they are doomed. The Sonnenfeldt Doctrine, perhaps packaged more adroitly, thrives.

Is the peace treaty between Israel and Egypt signed? Probably not. Carter's extraordinary stubbornness and his special relation with Sadat, including praying together, made it possible. It is especially difficult to imagine Gerald Ford conversing about Holy Scripture with the president of Egypt or the prime minister of Israel. In other words, no change in the Middle East: Israel surrounded on all sides by enemies.

Do the Russians go into Afghanistan? The Kremlin is less nervous about America. The military is against the invasion. Gromyko calms Brezhnev down and urges him not to risk the enormous propaganda success represented by the 1980 Moscow Olympics. Even if the appetite for the warm waters of the Indian Ocean wins out and the Russians go in, does the United States set in motion its vast support for the mujahideen, with Beijing's energetic cooperation? Unlikely.

Without the powerful pressures to uphold human rights and without the support for liberation movements in the communist camp, does the conclave of Cardinals elect Karol Wojtyla? I'm not sure.

On China, Ford and Deng have fewer common interests. Deng wants to draw closer to an America that takes a hard line toward Moscow. Ford and Kissinger want to avoid irritating Moscow. Deng will not travel to a Washington that is disinclined to break with Taiwan. Ford is disinclined.

In view of the fact that Carter's rhetoric was more about human rights than tanks and rockets, he has been perceived then and now as soft on American defense. The reality was different. Carter backed the modernization of many rocket systems and leaned on NATO countries to shore up the alliance's forces, both conventional and nuclear. Does Ford, in an alternative scenario, do the same?

It seems mind-boggling to assert that a different outcome to the 1976 presidential election could have prevented the downfall of the Soviet Union. Nevertheless, a case can be made that if not for an accumulation of factors unfavorable to Moscow—the Afghan war, Reagan's hardball policy, American support for human rights, John Paul II in the Vatican, and the Polish Solidarity movement—the Soviet empire would have held out longer. How long? That depends on how Gorbachev uses the time given to him. His rule falls in times of cheap oil. He doesn't have the money to keep up in the arms race and at the same time buy peace inside a moribund empire. If he could hold on longer, fate might smile upon him, just as it would smile upon Putin in 2004.

This is mere speculation, because the tape cannot be rewound—fortunately.

# CUBA FOR HIRE

**In June 1978, Fidel Castro accused Brzezinski of lying and manipulating President Carter.**

In May, Katangan rebel units invaded the Shaba province of Zaire. The American intelligence services reported that these units were trained and armed by the Cubans.

In a New York Times News Service interview with Castro by Jon Nordheimer, published in the June 10, 1978 edition of the *Chicago Tribune*, Castro denied with great passion these charges, and said that it had been the policy of his government to avoid "encouragement" of the Katangans since the cessation of the civil war in Angola in early 1976.

"It is not a half-lie," he said with regard to the charges. "It is an absolute, total, complete lie."

He was careful to avoid suggesting that Carter personally had taken a hand in producing what he called a "gross fabrication" about the Cuban role in Africa.

"It was a manufactured lie—manufactured in Brzezinski's office," Castro said. "I think Mr. Carter has been confused and deceived, but I do not think Mr. Carter has deliberately resorted to this himself." "Without doubt," Castro said, "People in his administration want to manufacture their own Gulf of Tonkin in order to intervene in Africa."

Castro offered to meet with President Carter to clear the air on this issue.

Carter did not take up Castro's offer and instead noted in a diary entry dated June 13, 1978 that "Castro has blamed all the problems concerning Cuba and the Shaba Province on Brzezinski. He's joined the Soviets and Israelis and everyone else—when they have a problem with me, to blame it on Zbig."

Three months earlier, Castro apparently had a different opinion of the national security adviser when he expressed a readiness to meet with him. Carter's diary entry from March 10 reads: "I had a report from a Cuban American dignitary who visited Castro that he's eager to meet with me or Brzezinski and is willing to be flexible on releasing the 2,500 political prisoners (to use his figure) and on the subject of Cuban involvement in Africa. We will approach this cautiously."

The Soviets and their allies had been testing America in Africa for several years. One-fourth of the entire Cuban army, 120,000 troops, was propping up the fragile Marxist regime in Angola. In 1978, Havana called up male reservists over the age of 40 for only the second time.

With Moscow footing the bill, the Cubans eased their unemployment woes—not only for the young and not only for men. Vilma Espin, head of the Federation of Cuban Women and wife of Fidel's brother, Raul Castro, proudly told a *Time* correspondent that

> at the height of the war in Angola, we had thousands of letters from women of all ages, including ones in their 70s, asking to go as cooks. One of the most important changes in Cuba since the revolution is that women who were afraid to go out of their houses 20 years ago are now requesting permission to go on internationalist missions. . . . Vice President Rodriguez admits that at first Cuba's civilian contingents abroad "looked like a kind of correctional institution, filled with delinquents, undesirables, homosexuals—even Jehovah's Witnesses. That was a distortion of our purpose. Some people falsified their

*papers or exchanged papers with their comrades so that they could go. Now we can pick and choose carefully, since we have no difficulty getting volunteers."* . . . *In proportion to its population, Cuba has more of its sons—and daughters—in Africa fighting for international Marxism than the U.S. had fighting against that cause at the height of its involvement in Viet Nam. Yet to date, Cuban battlefield fatalities have been light compared to American losses in Viet Nam.*

Mengistu Haile Mariam came from a poor family living in a village near the border with Sudan. Emperor Haile Selassie took note of him during a tour of the provinces, arranged for him to enroll at a military academy, and then sent him on two different occasions to study at the United States Army Command and General Staff College at Fort Leavenworth, Kansas, where the alumni include George C. Marshall, Douglas MacArthur, Dwight Eisenhower, and Omar Bradley, and the commandant from 2005 to 2007 was David Petraeus, the current head of the CIA. Mengistu reached the rank of major in the emperor's army. He led the military coup that, with communist support, toppled the ruler in 1974. He ordered that the emperor be immured beneath the marble floor tiles of the palace toilets, along with seventy relatives and members of his household. Mengistu espoused the lesson taught by every revolution in the world: In the process of renewal, victims are inevitable. He gathered all power into his own hands. Amnesty International estimates that his regime murdered half a million people in 1977-1978 alone. Mengistu remarked that "the revolution needs the blood of traitors." From that moment on, a wave of red terror swept through the country.

Facing threats of secession by Eritrea and a Somali-backed insurrection in the country's desert regions, Mengistu sought support in Moscow. The choice between Somalia, already dependent on the Soviets, or Ethiopia, with ten times the population and a location with access to strategic oil transport routes out of the Persian Gulf, was straightforward. The Mengistu regime signed a military pact with the Kremlin in May 1977. It was mostly about weaponry, instructors, and Cuban troops to regain the Somali-inhabited province of Ogaden. That was the moment when General Ochoa and General Petrov became comrades in arms and neighbors.

Divisional General Arnaldo Ochoa, a graduate of the Frunze Military Academy in Moscow—the Soviet equivalent of West Point—was already fighting at Fidel's side in the Sierra Maestra in 1957. He trained rebels in the Congo from 1967, and then, in one of Havana's most secret operations, and most costly in terms of human lives, he attempted to set up a leftist guerrilla movement in Venezuela. In 1975, Fidel shipped him off to Luanda. Already serving as Cuban deputy defense minister and a member of the party's central committee, he commanded Cuban units in Angola and won acknowledgment from both the Cuban authorities and the Soviet military. He accompanied Fidel on a secret 1977 trip to Ethiopia and remained behind to fight. In Addis Ababa, he shared quarters with his direct superior, General Vasily Ivanovich Petrov, as well as other Soviet generals.

Petrov also had some uncommon missions under his belt. During World War II he fought in the defense of Odessa, Sevastapol, and the Caucasus. Promoted to general in 1961, he received a second star in 1965 and commanded the units that skirmished with the Chinese in the Far East in 1969. He won his third star the following year, and received the fourth one that made him an army general in 1972. He commanded the armed forces in the Far East until 1976, when he became the first deputy commander of Soviet ground forces. It was General Petrov who took command of the Ethiopian campaign in Ogaden, envisioned as a recapitulation of the Cuban blitzkrieg in Angola. The Soviets were arming both sides in the conflict. In the end, the dimensions of their military aid to Ethiopia exceeded everything but the gigantic aid that they extended to Syria in October 1973, during the Yom Kippur war against Israel. Cuban forces in Ethiopia were estimated at 15,000 troops, along with 1,500 Soviet advisers. Nor were the other communist countries stinting with fraternal support. North Korea trained the "People's Militia," and the DDR helped with training and equipment; when the scale of communist aid to Ethiopia became apparent, Somalia broke off diplomatic relations with Moscow and expelled all Soviet citizens from its territory.

As Gates later recalled, United States intelligence estimates for the period January-April 1978 confirmed the accuracy of Brzezinski's view of the situation. Moscow saw a chance to strengthen its position in the most populous country of East Africa, build up its naval position in the Horn of Africa, lend ideological reinforcement to a sympathetic regime, and potentially eliminate the Somali leader, Siad Barre. The expansion of the Lourdes listening post in Cuba allowed the Soviets to monitor American communication satellites, military signals, and NASA activity at Cape Canaveral, as well as to eavesdrop on telephone conversations within the United States.

In the White House, Brzezinski was doing something he had been dreaming of. He was shaping, or as he puts it, "co-shaping" the policy of a dominant superpower. He was as well prepared for this as anyone could be. Furthermore, the world was at an important turning point. The dangerous ideological adversary—whose intentions and methods he had been studying since his youth and about whose plans he had no illusions—was gaining the upper hand. First, it broke America's atomic monopoly. Then it surprised America with its accomplishments in space. On one occasion already, in the case of Cuba, it had brought the world to the brink of a conflict with potentially unpredictable results. It had overrun

Brzezinski's wife's homeland, Czechoslovakia, with tanks in a way that proved it would not hesitate to satiate its appetite. Day after day, it probed America—its will, determination, and courage.

The president placed enormous trust in Brzezinski, who had no need to wrap anything in cotton wool. He did not need to play games. Yet there was one moment when he considered ditching everything and saying, "Enough!" The reason was Cuba.

The modernization of the Cuban armed forces led to a fresh American-Soviet dispute in 1978. The issue was Moscow's breaking of the 1963 settlement by supplying Cuba with new models of the MiG-23 that were capable of carrying nuclear weapons. The CIA detected these planes in November. Vance called in Ambassador Dobrynin to give him the news. Leaks reached the American press the following day. On November 16, Soviet Premier Kosygin told an American congressional delegation that the USSR had never broken the 1963 pact and the whole story about the MiG-23s was a fabrication.

Almost a year later, Cuba came up again. In late 1978 and early 1979, American intelligence reported on growing numbers of Soviet troops in Cuba, and also noted more MiG-23 sorties being flown by Russians. This made Brzezinski uneasy, while Vance thought there was no point raising objections that would inflame relations with the Kremlin. Zbig stood his ground, demanded new intelligence data, and informed Carter in the summer of 1979 that there was a Soviet brigade stationed in Cuba with its own barracks, staff, and all the signs of being battle-ready. Without Brzezinski's knowledge, an undersecretary of state informed Frank Church, the chairman of the Senate Foreign Relations Committee, about this. Regarded as a dove, Chuch was facing a tough re-election campaign and decided to use the issue to change his image. He called a press conference, and America heard the whole story before the administration had decided what stance to take. Vance suddenly donned his hawk costume, branded the status quo as unacceptable, and suggested demanding that Moscow withdraw the brigade. The public was disoriented and concerned, senators rushed to deliver belligerent statements, allusions were made to the Cuban Crisis of Kennedy's days, and the president decided to address the nation on the problem.

As it turned out, the Soviets had never fully left Cuba; the awareness of their presence, however, had slipped out of the intelligence community's institutional memory. Intense work was underway on Carter's speech when Senator Robert Byrd met Ambassador Dobrynin and gave him to understand that unless the Soviets withdrew their brigade, the fate of the SALT agreement would be endangered. Dobrynin retorted that the whole issue was a red herring because the unit had been stationed in Cuba for years. Brzezinski pressed for using the occasion to condemn the USSR for its African escapades and use of Cuban troops as surrogates for its own presence. Administration doves rang the alarm bell, labeling this as Cold War rhetoric. In his televised speech to the nation on October 1, Carter said that the Soviet unit stationed on Cuban territory was a matter of concern to America, but did not constitute a direct threat. This came as a blow to Brzezinski. He could not disguise his bitterness and disappointment. Moscow had admitted to violating the agreement, yet showed no intention of removing its troops. The world took note of precisely that passage in Carter's speech where the president stated that there was "no reason for a return to the Cold War." In his memoirs, Brzezinski wrote that

> *this was the only time that I ever thought seriously of the possibility of resigning. I felt so deeply about this that on October 4 I made what probably were the most disagreeable comments I ever made to the President in the course of our years; namely, that for the first time since World War II the United States told the Russians on several different occasions that we take great exception to what they are doing, that there will be negative*

*consequences if they persist in their acts, be it in Vietnam or in Iran or in the Middle East or in Africa, and more recently in Cuba, and then we did nothing about it. . . . The President looked quite furious, and told me that he had no intention of going to war over the Soviet brigade in Cuba. I responded by saying that I did not advocate that we go to war, but that we lay it on the line more explicitly in regard to Soviet adventurism around the world.*

The procedures had broken down and there was nothing to be either proud or satisfied about. In Congress, the crisis undermined confidence in both the administration and the USSR to a degree that weakened the chances for ratifying SALT II.

What fate awaited the protagonists of this tale?

General Petrov was supreme commander of Soviet ground forces from 1980 to 1985. he was awarded the title Hero of the Soviet Union in 1982 and promoted to Marshal of the Soviet Union a year later. After 1992, he was military adviser to the Ministry of Defense of the Russian Federation.

More dramatic destinies lay ahead for Ochoa and Mengistu.

Arnaldo Ochoa received the title Hero of the Revolution from Fidel in 1984. Five years later, Defense Minister Raul Castro nominated him to be head of the Cuban Western Army, equivalent to the third-highest post, after Fidel and Raul, in the Cuban military structure. This was when things became unexpectedly complicated.

During the course of what would seem to have been a routine vetting procedure, the revolutionary hero was accused of corruption not limited to trafficking in diamonds and ivory from Angola or arms in Nicaragua. Bribes were discovered from Colombian cocaine-trafficking gangs in exchange for access to Cuban territorial waters for dropping off and picking up shipments. Raul Castro, a close friend of Ochoa's, supposedly begged his comrade on various occasions to admit to everything and start a new life. Yet Ochoa allegedly refused to cooperate. He was then arrested and incarcerated in a prison near Havana. His best friends visited him there and urged him to express remorse in exchange for a lighter sentence, all in vain. A colonel in the security service, Tony de la Guardia, was also charged.

De la Guardia was a friend of the renowned Colombian writer, Gabriel Garcia Marquez, who won the 1982 Nobel Prize for novels including *One Hundred Years of Solitude*. Garcia Marquez dedicated his novel *The General in His Labyrinth*, a fictional account of the last days of Simon Bolivar, to the colonel accused of trading in cocaine. This resulted in violent revulsion in Latin America, with some taking it as besmirching the reputation of one of the continent's most important historical figures.

The trial was broadcast on television. Ochoa testified that he began committing his illegal acts out of an innocent need to buy guns and supplies for his units. The military court convicted him of treason. The prosecution argued that at least one of the pilots of the drug flights was under CIA contract, and that if it had been the Americans rather than the Cubans who uncovered the whole operation, it could have served as a pretext for invading the island. They also sketched a scenario in which, had the Cubans not exposed Ochoa's crimes, he could have been named head of the Western Army. This would have given the United States an excellent opportunity for blackmailing and controlling the person responsible for Cuban national security.

The Council of State unanimously approved the death sentence, the first time in communist Cuba that a popular and universally respected leader was officially condemned to die. While no one doubted that Ochoa and de la Guardia were in league with the Colombian gangsters, doubts arose over the timing and coverage of the trial. Not everyone regarded it as a coincidence that Ochoa's arrest closely followed a visit by Gorbachev.

It began, like in the good old days, with bear hugs, cannon salvos, and even a fifty-minute motorcade through the streets of Havana in an open Chaika limousine—the sort of thing that Castro usually avoided, but not when such a guest came to town. A visit the year before was called off because of the Armenian earthquake disaster, but Castro had warned in an armed-forces-day speech against both political experiments that undermined the leading role of the communist party and detente between the superpowers. "Everything is fine with our friendship, and everything is clear in our hearts, in our souls, and on our faces," *La Prensa Latina* quoted Gorbachev as telling journalists, according to the April 3, 1989 *New York Times*. Hearts and souls notwithstanding, things were less rosy with regard to Gorbachev's wallet. He arrived bearing not only reassurances of friendship, but also news of cuts in subsidies. In late 1991, just before the collapse of the USSR, he announced a unilateral decision to withdraw the 3,000-strong brigade from Cuba—the same one whose presence had been such a worry to Brzezinski a dozen years earlier.

Fidel Castro was a hardened opponent of Gorbachev's reforms. Ochoa was a charismatic figure with views said to be more liberal than those of the brothers Castro. He also had very close contacts with the Soviet leadership. This led to speculation that he could be an ideal leader for any coup d'etat, or Moscow's anointed in an operation similar to the changing of the guard that the KGB orchestrated in Kabul.

The Castro brothers were supposedly wary about narcotics. They must have known that their comrades were making money on the side, but they had no desire to get mixed up in anything big. Perhaps Ochoa and de la Guardia went beyond the permitted boundaries, or perhaps they had to be eliminated before they started talking.

The world was upside down. Gorbachev said no to Fidel Castro when he asked for money, and yes to Zbigniew Brzezinski when he wanted to visit the graves of the Polish officers murdered in Katyn.

Arnaldo Tomas "El Moro" Ochoa Sanchez was shot at an army base in west Havana on July 13, 1989. He reportedly asked to face the firing squad without a blindfold and to give the order to open fire himself, and both requests were supposedly granted. According to a less melodramatic account, the head of the Military Special Services, General José Luis Mesa Delgado, finished off Ochoa with a gunshot to the head—just as NKVD Captain Vasily Blokhin, later a general, did in the Lubyanka in 1937. The widow was informed later about an unmarked grave in a Havana cemetery.

The epilogue to Miriam Mengistu's story has not yet been written. As the country's dictator, he founded the Workers Party of Ethiopia in 1984. Two years later, he changed the constitution. He carried out a purge and the forced collectivization of agriculture, which led to a famine. His army numbered over 300,000 professional soldiers and was the largest in Africa. It consumed more than forty percent of the gross domestic product. He went to see Brezhnev at least once a year. Socialist Ethiopia even celebrated the same holidays as the Soviet Union. Mengistu saw Gorbachev as a traitor and his reforms as unworthy of the principles of Marxism.

In May 1991, as an offensive by opposition forces approached the capital, Mengistu fled to Zimbabwe. Afterwards, the Ethiopian authorities pleaded in vain for his extradition. On May 26, 2008, he was sentenced in absentia to the death penalty for the crime of genocide. His soldiers were notorious for refusing to turn the corpses of their terror victims over to relatives until they had been compensated for the cost of the ammunition used in the murder.

## Notes

Vilma Espin boasts about Cuban volunteers for service abroad: "Comrade Fidel Wants You," *Time*, July 10, 1978.

Brzezinski considers resigning: *Power and Principle*, pp. 351–352.

# THE SHAH CHECKMATED

The image of the more-than-year-long occupation of the United States embassy in Teheran burned into the memory like concentrated acid on delicate skin. It left a scar that only the sight of the World Trade Center towers collapsing could eclipse. It became a symbol of American humiliation and impotence. The fiasco of the attempt to free the hostages drove the final nail into the coffin of the Carter team's re-election dreams.

Brzezinski plays to win. He hates like hell to lose. If he does, it's always with style. But Iran was a shattering defeat in horrid style. Zbig always defends Carter and his White House years with conviction and passion. But there is no defending the Iran fiasco. Brzezinski doesn't even try.

Iran was above all a disaster for American intelligence. The country was crawling with American businessmen, advisers, military personnel, and spies, yet when push came to shove they all turned out to be blind and deaf. And following this intelligence catastrophe came an unbroken chain of errors: decisions that were off the mark, came too late, or never came at all. The intelligence failure caused situational disorientation. This made it hard to react to events. The lack of consensus among the main players paralyzed decision-making. Looking for heroes was pointless. Whose fault was it? Everybody's.

In November 1977, Mohammed Reza Shah Pahlavi, the ruler by the grace of God since 1941, flew to Washington to meet with Carter. Brzezinski was standing alongside on the White House lawn during the welcoming ceremony when everyone suddenly started weeping—not from emotion, but because of the tear gas the Washington police was using against demonstrators. It was not a good omen.

To the degree that the Shah secularized and modernized the country, he steadily lost the support of the Iranian clergy. The "White Revolution" he announced in 1963 envisioned agricultural reform, the nationalization of the forests, privatization of some state property, revision of the electoral laws, women's rights, permission for adherents of other faiths to hold public office, profit sharing in industry, and a campaign against illiteracy. Traditionalists, that is the hierarchy of powerful and privileged religious wise men, regarded the shah's initiative as dangerous. Ayatollah Ruhollah Khomeini issued a manifesto attacking the shah and America. That was how the Pahlavi-Khomeini feud began. Khomeini had to seek shelter in exile.

Later came years of conflict between the monarch and the traditional trading class known as the *bazaari*, developing ever close relations with Israel, the outlawing of the communist party, and a range of other controversial measures in an atmosphere in which the SAVAK intelligence agency used brutal methods against political opponents. The shah's position in Iran continued to erode, but America seemed not to see.

On his way to Warsaw on January 1, 1978, President Carter stopped off briefly in Teheran where he described the Shah's Iran as an "island of stability." Several days later, in the religious center of Iran, the security forces opened fire on demonstrators protesting against a scurrilous article aimed at Ayatollah Khomeini.

The summer of 1978 was a time of anxiety in Washington over the condition of the Shah's regime. Both the CIA and the embassy reassured the White House. Everything was fine. By the end of the year it wasn't. Facing revolution, the shah expected Carter's help. The shah of Iran was a great friend of America and Iran held a crucial place in Washington's Middle East policy, serving as both an important ally and a buffer between American and Soviet influences. In a November 4 telephone call, Brzezinski assured the shah of Carter's unwavering support. At the same time, the State Department felt the shah should leave the country regardless of what came after him. The signals being sent to the shah by the U.S ambassador in Teheran were hard to decode.

The ailing, disoriented monarch simply wanted the Americans to tell him what to do. Should he use the army or not? Stay or go? Form a civilian or a military government? Open fire on the demonstrators or not? He never got a straight answer because Washington had none to give. Carter was torn between Brzezinski and Vance. Brzezinski wanted the shah to use force. Vance thought the game was up, that the shah should turn over the reins sooner rather than later, and that this would ease tensions in the country.

Carter's emissary, Deputy Commander of US Forces in Europe Gen. Robert E. Huyser, flew to Teheran on January 8, 1979. The Iranian army high command wanted to know one thing: if they seized power and the Soviets tried to invade, could Iran count on American support? That was all. The rest, they said, they could take care of. The Soviets rubbed their hands in glee over what was going on in Iran and were ready to intervene military from two sides, from the Caucasus and from Afghanistan. American military intelligence viewed such a scenario as highly probable. The State Department and the CIA had their doubts.

In the NSC Weekly Report # 84 to the President, date January 12, 1979, Brzezinski writes about "a surprising degree of consensus" among the State Department, the Defense Department, the Joint Chiefs, the CIA and the NSA.

"Basically, this view holds that once the Shah has departed, Khomeini will return to the country. Khomeini will revert to his role as venerable sage, establishing the general parameters of political action but not involving himself in the details. The National Front will operate carefully within those general limits, but will have considerable freedom of maneuver for their own moderate foreign policy and military objectives, though they will have to tread carefully on the domestic scene. The military should be able to live with this arrangement. The only serious threat from the left would come if the Shah should remain and the present situation be permitted to continue.

This meeting reflected an astonishing measure of the degree to which American analysts have identified the Shah not only as part of the problem but as the entire problem. This is dangerous self delusion. (Brzezinski underlined—AL). To a surprising degree, we seem to have become captive to the demonology of the Iranian mobs, who believe that once the exorcism of the Shah's departure has been performed, all will be well. Nothing could be further from the truth. One can recognize the fact that the Shah has let the situation drift past the point of no return and still understand the prognosis for any successor regime is extremely poor.

The National Front is composed of a group of aging politicians who can agree on nothing. Khomeini has very strong ideas about the kind of Islamic Republic he intends to create, and he will be as able and uncompromising on that score as he has been to date."

President's comment on the memo reads: "Zbig. After we make joint decisions, deploring them for the record doesn't help me."

Carter tended to favor Vance's position that military intervention was the worst scenario. Huyser appeared in Tehran to tell the army that Carter wanted a democratic Iran. To the army, this meant they were being abandoned.

On January 16 the shah, exhausted by illness, decided that without American backing it was time to pack his bags. He flew off to Egypt, where President Anwar Sadat and Vice President Hosni Mubarak received him as a head of state. General Abbas Gharabani, chief of staff of the Iranian army, gave Khomeini—who had returned from exile a few weeks after Huyser's visit—a pledge that the army would remain in its barracks.

In his book *Veil: The Secret Wars of the CIA 1981-1987,* Bob Woodward tore Brzezinski to pieces. CIA Director Admiral Stansfield Turner told Woodward (A *Washington Post* reporter working for Ben Bradlee, whose wife Sally Quinn took such an interest in Brzezinski's zipper) that the National Security Adviser was responsible for the intelligence failures. The litany of sins was lengthy, to which we shall return in a moment, but also highly problematic. Woodward's version of Turner is completely different from Turner's own version of himself in *Burn Before Reading* (2005). Eighteen years elapsed between the two accounts. Either Woodward didn't like Brzezinski and thus heard what he wanted to hear, or Turner did a complete about-face. Nor can a third variant be ruled out: Woodward had a bone to pick with Brzezinski and decided to do a number on him, and Turner's memory later improved.

Woodward listens with great sympathy to the CIA boss's laments. Turner tries, successfully, to convince him that many of his problems as head of American intelligence can be traced back to Brzezinski, "who seemed to think that the CIA worked for him." When Turner stuck to his guns in a dispute with Brzezinski over an arms-control question, Brzezinski supposedly told him: "You are not the Supreme Court. You're not the fourth branch of government. You've got to decide who you work for."

> Brzezinski loved raw intelligence. The National Security Agency, which intercepted foreign communications, often

*provided him with transcripts of some head of states talking, or with the decoded political analysis that some foreign embassy in Washington had sent back to its capital. 'Did you see that intercept?' Brzezinski would ask. Turner felt that Brzezinski made the typical junior analyst's mistake, believing that it was possible to explain large events by isolated cables or intercepts. Too often the NSA picked up some blowhard, or a misinformed and self-important official, or an ambassador reporting more than he knew. Turner had written under the heading NSA: 'Uni-source analysis is dangerous.' . . . There had been a constant struggle with Brzezinski, who was at times predatory. 'You haven't got a single asset in the Soviet Union,' he once charged at the meeting with Turner's senior deputies.*

At another point, Brzezinski said that his former students at Columbia presented better analyses than the CIA.

"Carter and Brzezinski," says Woodward, "regarded intelligence as a tool, like a plumbing. When it didn't work, when the 'bug' was not instantly in place, or when the CIA could not foresee the future there was hell to pay. Turner realized, dimly at times, starkly at other times, that he was isolated both from his agency and from the President.

So what does Turner have to say in his book *Burn Before Reading*?

The Admiral admits that, on Iran, the CIA got it wrong right down the line.

*We had not appreciated how shaky the shah's political foundation was; did not know that the shah was terminally ill; did not understand who Khomeini was and the support his movement had; did not have a clue as to who the hostage-takers were or what their objective was; and could not pinpoint within the* embassy where the hostages were being held and under what conditions. As far as our failure to judge the shah's position more accurately, we were just plain asleep.

Further on, Turner writes that

> [i]n late December 1977, President Carter was in Tehran. He toasted the shah as being 'an island of stability' in an unstable area. We in the CIA were not aware that this was anything but the case. Eight months later, after rioting had broken out in Tehran several times, I received a draft of a National Intelligence Estimate that said that the shah would survive another ten years. I sent it back, insisting that we at least acknowledge that the shah had problems, as indicated by the sporadic rioting against him. It was egregious, that I did not insist on a thorough review of where the shah stood. Almost all of us in the national security establishment had been to Iran under the shah. We had not noticed any instability, as we were treated royally, but limited in where we could go and what we could see. The Iranians we met were urbane and wonderfully hospitable. And the shah had become an essential underpinning of U.S. policy in the Persian Gulf. Producing an intelligence estimate that the shah might not survive would have been seen as inviting that to happen. Even so, we should have been far more objective. President Carter, Zbigniew Brzezinski, and the national security staff were more so than we at the CIA. In late 1978, when the shah was still in power, I received a memo of reprimand from the president complaining about the quality of political intelligence he was receiving on Iran and the Middle East. This was a hard blow.

Turner and his CIA saw Khomeini as a harmless, harping cleric. The divisions within the administration on the question of Iran carried over into the question of what to do about the embassy takeover. Vance strongly opposed a military option to free the hostages. President Carter opted for negotiations but wanted to be prepared for a military solution as well. The White House was so afraid of the hostages coming to any harm that it did not send an aircraft carrier, which was already in the Indian Ocean, into the Gulf.

Then came the dispute over whether to admit the shah or not. Brzezinski was for and Vance against. When it turned out that the shah was terminally ill, Carter consented and the shah flew to America on October 23. Several days later, Brzezinski flew to Algeria to represent the United States at the 25th anniversary of that country's revolution. This was intended as a conciliatory gesture, because there was a collection of guests there with whom Brzezinski neither had to nor wanted to meet: Assad, Qaddafi, Arafat, Vietnamese General Giap, and Soviet Admiral Gorshkov. Brzezinski did meet with an Iranian government delegation of Prime Minister Bazargan and the foreign and defense ministers. They demanded that the Shah be turned over to face a tribunal in Tehran. In the words of Gates, who was present, Brzezinski stood up and said, "To return the Shah to you would be incompatible with our national honor." Although the meeting ended at this point, it had been friendly enough overall. The occupation of the American embassy in Teheran and the hostage crisis that sealed Carter's electoral defeat began several days later. Bazargani's government fell two weeks after that, in large part due to his meeting with Brzezinski.

Did Iran have to turn into a theocracy, extremely hostile toward America? To what degree did the contention between the moderate Vance and the hawk Brzezinski leave Carter in two minds and incapable of decisive action?

After the fiasco of the operation to free the hostages, which he had opposed, Cyrus Vance resigned. On his last day, he limped out of the president's office on a cane because of a gout attack. Gerald Rafshoon, Carter's media adviser, quipped: "Zbig bit him on the foot."

Brzezinski wrote in his memoirs:

> *Perhaps that disaster was historically inevitable, the Islamic fundamentalist wave too overpowering, and perhaps the Shah could never have been saved from either his own megalomania or, in the end, his paralysis of will. But my pained belief is that more could have been done by us on the America side. Historical determinism is only true after the fact.*

On February 16, 1979, he noted: "The first executions have already started, with four top generals being shot earlier today." And on February 20 he wrote: "A depressing story of chaos and confusion. The more I hear of what is going on, the more depressed I am over the fact that I did not succeed in getting the US government to approve and, if necessary, to initiate an Iranian military coup."

The dilemma then facing America was nothing new: to support a regime that violates human rights because it is a strategic ally, or to turn away from it because it does not respect basic American values? The former option has its advantages but at the cost of the loss of face and credibility among people who remember wrongs and suffering. The latter has costs for short-term American interests but carries the hope that, in the long run, a principled stance yields incomparably greater benefits. the hardest maneuver of all is switching from one option to the other, and America has never yet managed to pull it off in the Middle East. In Iran the sudden criticism of a longtime ally was still too little for the protesting masses, while the army chiefs, ready to take over, never got the signal that America would not permit the Soviets to invade Iran.

Iran turned out to be Carter's worst foreign-policy fiasco. The main ally in the Persian Gulf was lost. The unsuccessful operation to free the hostages cost him and Brzezinski a second term.

## Notes

Woodward's allegations of Brzezinski's poor relations with the intelligence community: *Veil: The Secret Wars of the CIA 1981–1987*, p. 28.

Turner on intelligence failures: Turner, *Burn Before Reading*, pp. 180, 181.

Brzezinski's refusal in Algeria to return the shah: Robert Gates, *From the Shadows. The Ultimate Insider's Story of Five Presidents and How They Won the Cold War*, p. 131.

"Zbig bit him": Jordan, p. 283.

"More could have been done": *Power and Principle*, p. 354.

Depressing news from Feb. 16, 1979: *Power and Principle*, p. 393.

# HUNTING FOR SPARROWS

Brzezinski's office on the third floor of the Center for Strategic and International Studies building at 1800 K Street in the center of Washington resembles a Who's Who photo gallery. There's a picture of Zbig with John Paul II, both smiling, both with joy in their eyes, gripping each other's hands like a pair of old friends who haven't seen each other for a long time and would willingly fall into an embrace if not for all the cameras and the protocol they've already broken. Zbig alone with a still-young President Lyndon B. Johnson, with Ronald Reagan, with Mikhail Gorbachev, with Jimmy Carter of course, and playing chess with Prime Minister Begin. I found one photo particularly intriguing. I have already seen it on Al Jazeera: Brzezinski in front of an honor guard of the Chinese People's National Liberation Army. He looks far more serious, or at least older, than when they received him with full honors in China in the 1970s. I ask him when this photo was taken. "Several years ago," Zbig replies. So what was the big occasion?

"This was the week that changed the world," said President Richard Nixon in a toast as he prepared to leave Shanghai at the end of his visit to China in February, 1972.

Both he and Kissinger, who laid the groundwork for the visit, had their chests puffed out proudly—they had broken the ice dividing

America from China. Nixon felt a gnawing fear, not unreasonable, that Kissinger would claim the laurels.

Margaret MacMillan asks in the introduction to her book *Nixon and Mao*, "Was the America president a supplicant, asking to come to China, or were the Chinese inviting him?" In her conclusion, after stating that the visit was "good for both countries," she remains uncertain: "Is it possible, though, to ask whether the United States was too eager and whether it gave away too much. . . . Should the Americans have handed over quite so much confidential material about the Soviets and, moreover, given the impression that the United States was eager to have an alliance with China against the Soviet Union?"

The ailing Mao feared Moscow. Only three years earlier, the Soviets had given him a licking on the Ussuri River. At a meeting with Japanese socialists in 1964, Mao had complained that Tsarist Russia took great swathes of territory from China in Siberia and the Far East, and China had never presented the bill. This made Khrushchev so furious that he refused to sign a border treaty that had already been negotiated. Tensions rose until the tanks appeared and blood finally flowed. In the fall of 1969 Soviet Prime Minister Alexei Kosygin stopped in Beijing on the way home from Ho Chi Minh's funeral to confer with his Chinese counterpart, Zhou Enlai. Relations were so frosty that the talks took place at the airport. China had been economically ruined by the Great Helmsman's ideas, crippled internally by the Cultural Revolution, and isolated from both the West and the communist camp.

"In their talks with the Americans, both during Kissinger's preliminary visits and now during Nixon's, the Chinese did not lay great stress on the Soviet Union. Occasionally they referred to 'our northern neighbor' or 'another big power,' or made jokes about polar bears."

Nixon hoped that China would help him disentangle himself from Vietnam, while China hoped that America would reject

Taiwan and treat it as part of the People's Republic. "History also proves that Taiwan has belonged to China for more than a thousand years—a longer period than Long Island has been part of the US," MacMillan quotes Zhou as telling Kissinger in 1972 in *Dangerous Games: The Uses and Abuses of History*. "In fact," she corrects him, "history proves no such a thing." Taiwan "was too far across the sea for most Chinese dynasties to bother with. Only the last dynasty, the Qing, tried to assert some control, partly because the island had become a refuge for pirates and rebels."

*In Joint Communiqué signed in Shanghai on February 28, 1972, the Chinese side reaffirmed its position: the Government of the People's Republic of China is the sole legal government of China; Taiwan is a province of China which has long been returned to the motherland; the liberation of Taiwan is China's internal affair in which no other country has the right to interfere; and all U.S. forces and military installations must be withdrawn from Taiwan. The Chinese Government firmly opposes any activities which aim at the creation of "one China, one Taiwan," "one China, two governments," "two Chinas," an "independent Taiwan" or advocate that "the status of Taiwan remains to be determined."*

The US side declared: The United States acknowledges that all Chinese on either side of the Taiwan Strait maintain there is but one China and that Taiwan is a part of China. The United States Government does not challenge that position. It reaffirms its interest in a peaceful settlement of the Taiwan question by the Chinese themselves. With this prospect in mind, it affirms the ultimate objective of the withdrawal of all US forces and military installations from Taiwan. In the meantime, it will progressively reduce its forces and military installations on Taiwan as the tension in the area diminishes.

This "constructive ambiguity," in the words of Henry Kissinger, would continue to hinder efforts for complete normalization.

The "historical opening" didn't change much. After the thaw came no spring. The Nixon-Kissinger duet was cautious, afraid of ruining their relations with Moscow; Beijing viewed detente warily.

When Watergate forced Nixon to resign, Gerald R. Ford hurried to assure Mao that normalizing relations with China was his highest priority. No deeds followed this declaration.

At the end of 1974, Kissinger traveled to Beijing shortly after the Ford-Brezhnev disarmament summit in Vladivostok, which had itself been a tactless choice of venue. Seventy kilometers from the Chinese border, Vladivostok had belonged to China 115 years earlier. Now it was the home base of the Soviet Pacific Fleet. In Beijing's eyes, holding the summit in Vladivostok signaled American consent for the Soviet role of Far East superpower. Taking the place of the gravely ill Zhou, Deng Xiaoping faced Kissinger. Instead of refined Parisian manners and diplomatic nuance, that meant hard arguments and obstinate positions, punctuated by regular resort to the spittoon. Deng pressed the Taiwan issue while Kissinger argued that America could not suddenly cut itself off from a partner it had so long been tied to. Deng showed no interest in sentiment. He lectured: The Soviet Union was stronger militarily than the United States and Europe combined. Because Moscow needed wheat and was industrially backward, it could not stand a prolonged war. Weren't we supposed to castrate the Polar Bear together? If we want to demonstrate to the world that there is authentic rapprochement between America and China, then Defense Secretary James Schlesinger should come to Beijing. This was a double blow to Kissinger. In the first place, Schlesinger was a critic of detente as Kissinger understood it and felt that America was too soft with Moscow. Second, an invitation to him would call Kissinger's position into question. In order to avoid returning home empty handed, Kissinger wheedled an invitation for Ford to visit Beijing out of

Deng, who set harsh conditions: break off relations with Taiwan, withdraw American troops from the island, and annul the mutual defense pact. Kissinger agreed to everything, even while knowing deep down that the terms were unacceptable.

Zhou died in January 1976 and Mao less than a year later. Frustrated with the lack of progress, the Chinese invited Nixon, now as a private citizen, sending an aircraft for him. Kissinger admitted that he never believed in the normalization of relations with China.

Several months later, people who did not discount such a possibility moved into the White House. Carter was initially busy with the Middle East and the Soviets above all. Moscow was testing him, trying to find out how far they could push him, what language to speak to him, and which arguments to use. When the Siberian chill blew through the first exchange of letters with Brezhnev due to intransigence over human rights, Carter began thinking of a turn toward China.

Brzezinski was ready. When he arrived at the White House, he reached out for help from Michel Oksenberg, a prominent China expert whose first assignment was to analyze what the previous two administrations had done. Brzezinski edited his report, "What Next with China," and sent it to the president. It caused a storm. Vance sharply reminded Brzezinski who was in charge of foreign policy. This was naive: Carter respected Vance, but he both respected and liked Brzezinski. Furthermore, it was Brzezinski, not Vance, who spent at least an hour a day with the president.

Brzezinski had long before moved past the point of regarding the Moscow-Beijing conflict as a family squabble. The Soviets and the Chinese genuinely hated each other, and Zbig did not intend to leave the China card in the drawer. He wanted to play it and he found two partners who were also willing to do so. The first was his staffer Oksenberg. The second was Leonard Woodcock, the former United Auto Workers president who had helped Carter win Michigan, earning presidential appreciation and appointment as head of the United States Liaison Office in Beijing.

Carter wanted to cut a deal which would permit a real relationship with China. Vance traveled to Beijing to convey the president's intentions, but he was too timid to appeal to the Chinese animus towards Moscow and did not convince the Chinese—perhaps because he had his own reservations about the step.

Soon after, following a meeting with the leader of Singapore, Lee Kuan Yew in which the Singaporean statesman urged greater determination in dialogue with China, Brzezinski asked Oksenberg, "Do you think you could get me an invitation to China?" Oksenberg was over the moon: "Jesus, Zbig, of course I could. They would love to have you."

At a white House meeting several days later, when the highest ranking Chinese diplomat in Washington was saying farewell to the vice president and the secretary of state at the end of his appointment, he declared that the Chinese People's Republic was delighted to invite Zbigniew Brzezinski to visit Beijing. Vance and his state department entourage were thunderstruck. They feared that a sudden rapprochement with Beijing, especially under Brzezinski's baton, would complicate disarmament negotiations. For Vance, SALT II was an overriding priority, so he was ready to torpedo anything that could impede it. Brzezinski could care less about putting the Kremlin's nose out of joint. To the contrary—and Deng felt the same way.

Zbig accepted the invitation but still needed the green light from the president. Vance felt that he should be the one to visit Beijing. Zbig lobbied hard. When he got his way, Richard Holbrooke, Vance's deputy for Asian affairs, attempted to fill Brzezinski's traveling party with state department regulars. According to Patrick Tyler's account, Holbrooke received a dawn phone call from an irascible Brzezinski who warned him that, if he persisted, Brzezinski would throw him off the airplane.

When I asked Brzezinski about the incident, he referred me to a letter Jimmy Carter sent in 1999 to Foreign Affairs, reacting to P. Tyler's article about the process of normalizing diplomatic relations with China, under the title "The (Ab) normalization of U.S.-Chinese Relations."

Carter wrote:

> "When I decided in 1978 to move on the China issue, my policy was well understood by all my key associates, and I properly sent Secretary of State Cyrus Vance to Beijing to make my position clear to the Chinese. The visit was a disappointing failure, but I decided to press forward, and in May 1978 I sent Brzezinski to make another effort to present my views to Vice Premier Deng Xiaoping and Chairman Hua Guofeng. He had a very successful visit, having obviously established good rapport with the Chinese leaders. From then on, I was leery of channeling my proposals through the State Department, because I did not feel that I had full support there and it was and is an enormous bureaucracy that is unable and sometimes unwilling to keep a secret. . . . So far as I know even now, my national security adviser never departed from the instructions I gave him, almost of which were discussed in our weekly meetings. . . . which included the secretaries of state and defense. Secretary Vance was conversant with every dispatch we sent and had constant access to me, so I did not give much weight to his disgruntled subordinates in the State Department, some of whom had been a constant source of complaints to the news media regarding the national security adviser's having too much influence over foreign policy."

So Brzezinski did indeed remove the diplomats from the picture, but did so on the strength of a presidential directive.

When in May 1978, Brzezinski flew to Beijing, he carried written instructions from Carter, which he had in fact drafted himself with Oksenberg's assistance:

> *Your basic goal should be to convey to the Chinese our determination to seek peace with the Soviets, to compete effectively with the Soviets, to deter the Soviet military challenge, and to protect our interests and those of our friends and allies. . . . You should then share with the Chinese my view of the nature of the Soviet threat. To state it most succinctly, my concern is that the combination of increasing Soviet military power and political shortsightedness, fed by big-power ambitions, might tempt the Soviet Union both to exploit local turbulence (especially in the Third World) and to intimidate our friends in order to seek political advantage and eventually even political preponderance. That is why I do take seriously Soviet action in Africa and this is why I am concerned about the Soviet military buildup in Central Europe. I also see some Soviet designs pointing towards the Indian Ocean through South Asia, and perhaps to the encirclement of China through Vietnam (and even perhaps someday through Taiwan).*

There follows a long list of American foreign-policy goals including strengthening NATO and cooperating more closely with Japan and China, while simultaneously engaging in "comprehensive and genuinely reciprocal detente with the Soviet Union."

> *You should share with the Chinese our analysis of internal Soviet weaknesses (both economic and political) and of their external difficulties (notably their waning ideological appeal, and the continued hostility of East Europe. In so doing, do not betray confidences nor take an anti-Soviet posture. You might indicate in this overall context that the United States does not*

*object to the more forthcoming attitude which our allies are adopting in regard to trade with China in technology-sensitive areas. We have an interest in a strong and secure China—and we recognize and respect this interest. . . . You might indicate informally to the Chinese that the United States is planning to further reduce its military presence in Taiwan this year, to widen the opportunities for the commercial flow of technology to China, to increase direct contacts on a regular and perhaps scheduled basis for our mutual advantage, and to invite Chinese trade and military delegations to visit the United States.*

The man who actually ruled China from 1978 without ever formally holding the posts of party secretary or premier was Deng Xiaoping. He had just turned 15 when with a group of other Chinese students he travelled to France. Older colleagues including Zhou Enlai won him over to Marxism and he attended the Moscow Sun Yat-sen University. Many years later, historians stated that Deng and many of his fellow Chinese communists had never really been Marxists but rather nationalist revolutionaries who wanted to restore China to its deserved place in the world. For them, joining the revolution was more an instrument than a declaration of faith. Immediately after the founding of People's China, Deng was finance minister and deputy premier. In 1961 he enunciated the motto that embodied his pragmatism: "It doesn't matter if the cat is black or white, as long as it catches the mouse." He said this at a time when the color of the cat mattered a great deal in China. Although Deng led the Chinese delegation to the talks with Khrushchev in 1963 that confirmed the Great Split and tried to rescue the Chinese economy after the Great Leap Forward, he was not spared during the Cultural Revolution. His son was tortured and thrown out of a fourth-floor window, which left him paralyzed.

Brzezinski was aware that Beijing regarded the Carter administration as soft on Moscow. That is why he used his talks with the head of the Chinese foreign ministry, which lasted over three hours, to talk about shared strategic goals and Carter's desire to reinforce NATO and rebuild America's military potential.

On May 21, 1978, he met for over two hours with Deng. In the White House memorandum on the conversation we read that Deng made things crystal clear: "There is only one China. We will not accept two Chinas, or one-and-a-half Chinas in any form. Another question is to ask China to undertake the commitment to solve the issue of Taiwan by peaceful means. And we refused because the liberation of Taiwan is an internal affair of China in which no country has the right to interfere. As to when and how we resolve this question, it is China's own business."

Brzezinski: "In our relationships we will remain guided by the Shanghai communiqué, by the principle that there is only one China and the resolution of the issue of Taiwan is your problem. However, at the same time we have certain domestic problems and certain historical legacies that we will have to overcome.... That is why we will have to find some formula which allows us to express our hope and our expectation regarding the peaceful resolution of the Taiwan issue, though we recognize that this is your own domestic affair and that we do so in the spirit of the Shanghai communiqué. This consideration must be borne in mind when resolving the issue of normalization and when defining the full range of relations during the historical transitional period of our relationship with the people on Taiwan..."

The exchanges between Deng and Brzezinski on the issues regarding relations with Moscow show that the Chinese leader was clearly trying to put the US and Carter's National Security Advisor on the defensive, in effect arguing that the United States was excessively accommodating to the Soviet Union. It was almost an attempt of a reply of the 1974 meeting with Kissinger. "I knew about that encounter—says Zbig—and I felt that

I should not let him get away with it if he were to try it against Carter and me."

Deng on US-Chinese commercial relations: " . . . pending the normalization, such relations are bound to be limited and you yourselves are restricted. Perhaps I think you have the fear of offending the Soviet Union. Is that right?"

ZB: "I can assure you that my fear of offending the Soviet Union is rather limited. . . . As far as being afraid to offend the Soviet Union, I would be willing to make a little bet with you as to who is less popular in the Soviet Union—you or me . . . "

Deng: "To be candid with you, whenever you are about to conclude an agreement with the Soviet Union it is the product of concession on the US side to please the Soviet side."

ZB: "I must say that I don't quite agree with that. . . . We are not naïve in dealing with the Soviet Union. For the last thirty years it has been the United States which has opposed the Soviet agenda and the Soviet hegemonic designs and that is roughly twice as long as you have been doing it, so we have a little bit of experience in this. . . . President Carter when speaking of détente always uses two words over and over again. It has to be reciprocal and comprehensive. Behind these two words is deliberate political meaning. Reciprocal means that the Soviets cannot act differently to us than we can to them."

The next day, Brzezinski, accompanied by Woodcock, and Oksenberg, met in the Great Hall of the People, with Chairman Hua Kuo-Feng, Mao's formal successor. Zbig handed him a present from Carter, with a note that said: "To Chairman Hua, a piece of the moon for you and the people of China, symbolic of our joint quest for a better future. Jimmy Carter."

Hua said: "We must work together to cope with Soviet social imperialism. . . . We are certainly aware of the fact that the Soviet Union is bent on subjugating China. Therefore, we must raise our vigilance."

To that Brzezinski answered:

*I might also suggest to you that there is perhaps a philosophical difference in the approach to China on the part of President Carter, myself, and others, and on the approach on the part of President Nixon, Mr. Kissinger, and others. The accomplishment of Mr. Nixon and Mr. Kissinger in opening the dialogue with China was an historical accomplishment of great importance, which we value very highly. It was initiated during the Vietnamese War. Later during the Watergate crisis there was an element of historic pessimism involved in it. There was a fear that the United States was going down on the scale of history and that this had to be balanced by a relationship with China against the Soviet Union.*

*We do not underestimate the Soviet threat but we feel that the Soviet Union also suffers from many historical weaknesses. We are fundamentally optimistic about the long-term prospects of our competition with the Soviet Union. We think our friendship with you is useful in this competition but more importantly we think our friendship with you is a central part of our foreign policy as we try to shape a world which is truly cooperative, a word organized for the first time in its total history on the basis of independent states and therefore a world in which new political and social relationships have to emerge.*

*We therefore feel that our relationship with China is of historic significance. It is an enduring relationship. It has long-term strategic importance. It is not only a tactical anti-Soviet expedient. If the Soviet Union remains a threat, if it persists in its hegemonistic designs, we want to cooperate with you in resisting them: but if we succeed in accommodation to some extent, if SALT reduces Soviet strategic danger, we nevertheless feel that for global reasons, for historical reasons, we wish to have a relationship of ever closer friendship and cooperation*

> with China because you are a major, vital force in world affairs, whether the SU is peaceful whether the Soviet Union is peaceful or aggressive, friendly or hostile to the United States. My personal guess is that the Soviet Union will remain hostile and aggressive for some time to come.
> Hua: May I interrupt for a moment?
> Brzezinski: Please.
> Hua: China also looks at our relations with the US in a long-term strategic perspective . . . In our argument with Dr. Kissinger, we said to him that you should not, the United States should not go to Moscow on the shoulder of China. In other words, the US should not use China as a pawn in order to improve its relationship with the SU.
> Brzezinski. I agree with that. . . .
> On the question of normalization, you have used the phrase "If President Carter has made up his mind," things can be so easy. I think it would be probably more appropriate to say "Since President Carter has made up his mind" it should prove possible for things to be easy. The word "if" is inappropriate in view of the fact that in the course of the past two or three days I have already said three or four times that President Carter has made up his mind."
> Hua: We will observe the actual action.
> Brzezinski: One can make up one's mind to marry a girl but implementation sometimes requires overcoming some obstacles.

Brzezinski and Deng hit it off from the start. Their shared view of the Soviet danger cemented their partnership, which lasted until the Chinese leader's death. "A man tiny in size, but great in his boldness, Deng immediately appealed to me. Bright, alert, and shrewd, he was quick on the uptake, with a good sense of humor, tough, and very direct. After talking to him, I realized better why he had survived all the vicissitudes of his political career, but even more importantly, I was impressed by his sense of purpose and drive. Here was a political leader who knew what he wanted and with whom one could deal," wrote Brzezinski in his memoirs. Deng founded a cult of Brzezinski in China, as a result of which serving or retired presidents, premiers, or defense ministers receive him there to this day.

During a meeting at the US Institute of Peace in March 2012, Brzezinski recalled that

> *The conversations with Deng were very direct. As I read the transcripts of the Nixon—Mao, Kissinger—Zhou Enlai discussions they occasionally were more analytical, you could sense that there was a probing. With Deng it was much more direct. Sometimes some were sarcastic on his side, or provocative, to "smoke out," perhaps, our position. But, in the course of these discussions I have to say that in a strange sort of a way a kind of personal bond developed between us. I actually began to like him in addition to respect him.*

One recalcitrant item on the list of unsolved problems was arms sales to Taiwan. Recognizing China was one thing, but turning off the tap on Taipei from one day to the next was another. How could the Mutual Defense Treaty be annulled? Would Congress go along? Over our dead bodies, said Barry Goldwater and other conservatives.

Deng understood Carter's problems; he also had a surfeit of his own. The Soviet comrades came to the aid of both sides. On November 4, 1968, Moscow and Hanoi inked a treaty of friendship and cooperation. Deng took this as evidence of the building of an anti-Chinese alliance. He needed America more than ever. During a meeting with a Japanese parliamentary delegation on November 18, he said that he expected the strengthening of relations with

America; it would take "two seconds" to accomplish this and he could then travel to the United States.

The controversy over continued US arms sales to Taiwan, as it turned out, was not resolved to the full satisfaction of Beijing, and challenged the ultimate success of Brzezinski's effort until the very last minute. On December 15, 1978, the day the White House was to announce normalization, Brzezinski learned from the US Ambassador in Beijing that Deng was assuming that Washington would discontinue armed sales to Taiwan after their suspension for one full year during. During that time, Deng assumed, the United States would be terminating, in keeping with established commitments, their defense arrangements with Taiwan. "At our end, says Brzezinski, we were of the view that we would discontinue these arrangements while terminating formal diplomatic relations with Taiwan, but that we were retaining the right to continue them thereafter, though hopefully at diminishing levels."

"Ambassador Woodcock recommended that morning—recalls Brzezinski—that we simply let this issue pass and go ahead with the announcement, without clarifying the disagreement with the Chinese. I took the view that we better clarify it even if it should produce a disruption, because it would be worse if we announced the agreement and then had a serious collision which would discredit the entire effort. Accordingly, I instructed Woodcock to clarify our point of view to Deng. Deng was outraged, claimed that this was not what we had verbally agreed, but eventually gave in and decided to go ahead with the communiqué in full knowledge of how we were interpreting our commitments to Taiwan."

On December 15, 1978, Carter stood before the television cameras and stunned the world by announcing the establishment of diplomatic relations between the United States and the People's Republic. This step was not aimed at anyone, he said. The joint communiqué, however, stated that America and China were standing shoulder to shoulder against attempts at hegemony. The

Kremlin had no need of cryptanalysts to figure out what was going on. Brezhnev rejected Carter's invitation to visit Washington. Salt II landed in the icebox—perhaps the same one where Brezhnev's favorite vodka, a present from Dobrynin to Brzezinski, was already chilling.

On January 28, 1979, Brzezinski poured the vodka while entertaining Deng for supper at his McLean home during the first visit by a Chinese communist leader to Washington. At some point the host remarked that opposition from the right-wing Republicans had made normalizing relations with Beijing costly for Carter. "I asked him facetiously whether he had similar difficulties in China. In a flash, Deng responded: 'Yes, I did; there was some opposition in the province of Taiwan!'"

In his discussions with Carter, Deng criticized Soviet actions in South Asia and the Middle East while calling for American-Chinese cooperation against Moscow. The fact that Deng's visit to Washington had been preceded by his prolonged talks with Brzezinski made it unnecessary to mince words.

At a private meeting on February 6, 1979, attended by Mondale, Vance, and Brzezinski in addition to the president, Deng spoke of his need to teach the Vietnamese a lesson in reprisal for what he regarded as their overweening ambition. On the following day, Carter counseled moderation but without warning Deng against aggression or threatening to break off the normalization process—nothing, that is, beyond delicate moralizing. Forty-eight hours later, the CIA reported that there were fourteen Chinese divisions on the border with Vietnam and more arriving. Less than two weeks after that, the Chinese crossed the border and appeared to be heading for Hanoi. Battle-tested and better armed, the Vietnamese put up resistance. Moscow's reaction was the great unknown.

Would the Soviets rush to aid their ally Vietnam, or prefer not to risk a fight with the Chinese? Aside from arms shipments, Moscow barely lifted a finger. Beijing withdrew its troops, but the Chinese made their political point nonetheless. Hanoi immediately stepped up military cooperation with the Soviets, but Deng had achieved his goal.

When the Americans offered to cooperate in collecting and sharing intelligence on the Soviets, the Chinese leader assented. The Khomeini regime had deprived the Americans of two important posts in northern Iran that monitored Soviet missile tests. Deng and Brzezinski agreed during their talks to cooperate in building a center in western China to fill this role. Admiral Turner, head of the CIA, flew to Beijing on a super-secret mission, just before the handover of power to the Reagan team, in order to put the finishing touches on the deal.

Five years later, in December 1983, I met Zbig over supper at the Falls Church home of a common friend. Our host for the evening was a retired Air Fore General who had been a friend of Brzezinski's since the 1950s, William Y. Smith, the former deputy commander in chief of the US European Command. His wife Maria, like Muszka Brzezinska, was of Czech descent; they had been roommates at Wellesley. That was when Zbig told me about the moment captured in his famous photo with John Paul II.

The Reagan presidency was in its third year and new tensions had arisen with the Soviets, who had shot down Korean Airlines Flight 007 after mistaking it for a spy plane. Reagan was considering a new anti-missile defense system that the media had christened "Star Wars."

I asked Brzezinski what he thought of Reagan's foreign policy, the Star Wars idea, and forcing the Kremlin into an arms race. He smiled. "I recently returned from Beijing and I asked Deng Xiaoping exactly the same question. He replied by asking me if I knew how the Chinese hunt sparrows. I was taken somewhat aback, even though I was used to how rarely wise Chinese people give a straight answer. When I replied that I did not know, Deng enlightened me: We don't let them perch on a branch. We keep chasing them so that they have no time to rest. That was how the Chinese leader expressed his approval for Reagan's policy."

## Notes

Kissinger's 1974 trip to Beijing: Patrick Tyler, *A Great Wall: Six Presidents and China: An Investigative History*, pp. 193–200.

"Jesus, Zbig, of course I could": Tyler, *A Great Wall*, p. 248.

Brzezinski's dawn phone call to Holbrooke: Tyler, *A Great Wall*, p. 252.

Carter's instructions to Brzezinski for the Beijing negotiations: *Power and Principle*. Annex I, pp. 549–555.

"A man tiny in size . . . ": *Power and Principle*, p. 212.

Deng's quip at the supper table: *Power and Principle*, p. 406.

# VIENNA 1979—VIENNA 1959

The Habsburg Joseph II, Holy Roman Emperor, King of Hungary, Bohemia, Dalmatia, Croatia, Slavonia, Galicia and Lodomeria, Archduke of Austria, Duke of Burgundy, Lorraine, etc., called Wolfgang Amadeus Mozart's *The Abduction from the Seraglio* the first national opera. It was performed in Vienna more than any other. On a June evening in 1979, Jimmy Carter and Leonid Brezhnev left after the second act. They were both tired out—Carter by a long transatlantic journey and jet lag, Brezhnev by life.

For several months before their first meeting, the talk was not so much about the disarmament treaty, missiles and bombers and how to verify them, or which side was telling the truth and which side dissimulating, as about whether medical considerations would permit the encounter to go ahead. The 72-year-old leader of the USSR suffered from countless ailments that could not be concealed in public. He had trouble speaking and was sometimes incomprehensible. One day he seemed to be in tolerably good condition and the next he was unsteady on his feet. Ambassadors waiting in the receiving line exchanged observations after shaking his hand—was his grip firm or weak, was his hand trembling or not?

Brezhnev fit into the tradition of Soviet leaders who could be removed from power by death alone. A series of strokes paralyzed

Lenin in his final years, helping facilitate Stalin's scramble to the top. Once adroit and brutal, Lenin spent his final years complaining that Stalin was "uncivil" and suggesting that his comrades in the Political Bureau strip him of the post of general secretary of the party. Stalin, in turn, was convinced that he was dying as the result of a plot by Jewish doctors; he made his sickness not only a pretext for a bloody new purge and refused in his paranoia to be seen by doctors when the blood vessels in his brain were beginning to burst. Khrushchev was the first head of the party to lose power—hardly at his own wish—while he was still alive.

A seriously ill leader is, of course, not a Soviet invention. Had Roosevelt been healthier, the Viennese might never have been shocked by the presence of Red Army soldiers. As it was, they had to put up with them every day for ten years.

As Brzezinski recalled in his memoirs, of the many foreign policy debates within the Carter Administration, the one over policy toward the Soviet Union was the most prolonged and intense. It raised basic questions regarding relations with the allies, diplomacy toward the Middle East, but also "fundamental issues concerning the nature of our defense posture and nuclear strategy."

"The Soviets," he wrote, "had gained broad strategic parity (having obtained in SALT I American acceptance of Soviet superiority in certain categories of strategic weaponry) and had become more daring in exploiting openings in the Third World. Soviet reliance on Cuba as a military proxy in Africa was a particularly bold gambit, and it was paying off. In general, the sustained Soviet strategic and conventional buildup posed the threat that by 1985 Moscow might attain military superiority over the United States—notwithstanding Mr. Kissinger's casual dismissal in 1972 of the importance of such superiority."

As early as February 1976, well before the presidential election, Brzezinski spelled out in a memo to Carter the fundamentals of his approach to the US-Soviet relations in the following terms:

1. *The East-West détente is desirable, but it false to argue—as Kissinger has—that the only alternative to it is a war. The détente relationship is by its very nature a mixed one. It combines elements of both competition and cooperation.*

2. *Only a more comprehensive and a more reciprocal détente can enhance peace and promote change within the Communist system. The purpose of détente ought to be precisely such a twofold goal: détente should seek to avoid war, but in doing so it ought to be an instrument of peaceful change. Unless the latter takes place, we can never be certain that the former is enduring.*

3. *It is in the Soviet interest to keep détente limited and rather one-sided. In fact, the Soviets so interpret it quite explicitly. In a number of comments, the Soviet leaders have openly stated that the détente is meant to promote the "world revolutionary process," and they see the American-Soviet détente not only as a means of preserving peace but also as a way of creating favorable conditions for the acquisition of power by Communist parties, especially given the so-called aggravated crisis of capitalism.*

4. *In seeking to use détente for domestic purposes, both Nixon and Kissinger have oversold it as having already laid the basis for "generation of peace." Moreover, they have adopted a stance of moral indifference, as exemplified in the recommendation to the President that he refrain from receiving Solzhenitsyn."*

In describing what a comprehensive and reciprocal détente would mean in practice, Brzezinski stated, among other conditions, that "[t]here should be continued efforts to reach agreements with the Soviet Union on arms control, and there should be particularly an effort made to lower the present SALT ceilings. The ceilings are too high and they make possible not only further weapons deployment but they also breed mutual insecurities."

In strictly protocol terms, SALT II should have been signed in Washington. However, the Soviets insisted on neutral Vienna. Brezhnev's health was the official reason, but the Kremlin also wanted to distance itself physically and symbolically from Carter's domestic problems and possible Senate rejection of the treaty.

When the Soviet Union became a nuclear power, Moscow not only grew more self-confident but also understood the danger of mutual destruction. As Khrushchev put it, war was not a "fatalistic inevitability."

In his book, *Khrushchev Remembers: The Last Testament*, published in 1974, three years after the author's death, the former Soviet leader quotes himself:

> *I remember President Kennedy once stated that the United States had the nuclear missile capacity to wipe out the Soviet Union two times over, while the Soviet Union had enough atomic weapons to wipe out the United States only once . . . When journalists asked me to comment . . . I said jokingly, "Yes, I know what Kennedy claims, and he's quite right. But I'm not complaining . . . We're satisfied to be able to finish off the United States first time round. Once is quite enough. What good does it do to annihilate a country twice? We're not a bloodthirsty people."*

Peaceful coexistence became an alternative to mutual annihilation, which did not for a moment diminish in the eyes of the Kremlin the imperative for weapons of mass destruction.

This was the first summit since the meeting between Brezhnev and Ford in Vladivostok in 1974. Inaugurated by Nixon and Brezhnev beneath the crystal chandeliers of the Kremlin in 1972, detente was in poor shape. Between the Soviet nuclear arsenal, meddling in Africa, and the demise of the Shah, the Americans had enough to fret over. Brezhnev regarded Carter as weak and disoriented, but found his harping on human rights irritating. Then there was the morbidly anti-Soviet Brzezinski, forever whispering in Carter's ear to remind him about his ideological wards, the dissidents. Washington, for its part, was not sure whether the Soviet leader's health made any negotiations possible, how long Brezhnev would hang on, or who would succeed him. The meeting was expected to clarify many issues but settle few of them, beyond what the two counties' negotiators had agreed in Geneva.

The Soviets wanted "no surprises," and they wished the meetings to be brief. "In a sudden burst of candor," recalled Brzezinski, "Dobrynin [the Soviet Ambassador in Washington—AL] one day took me aside and reiterated the Soviet desire to limit all discussions to SALT, adding: 'The fact of the matter is that Carter knows so much more on all these issues than Brezhnev that Brezhnev will be on the defensive and embarrassed if Carter presses him on all of them. Stick to one or two major issues, and don't embarrass the old man. On such matters as encryption, if Carter makes him understand how important it is to ratification, Brezhnev might be helpful three or four months from now.'"

Brzezinski's approach to the summit differed from Vance's. In a memo to the President, a week before the Vienna summit, the Secretary of State stressed that "the primary focus of your exchanges with Brezhnev should be to reaffirm the basic framework of US-Soviet relations, which is based on substantial common interest in strategic stability, mutual acceptance of the status quo in the developed world and avoidance of confrontation in dealing with the Third World." "This passage," says Brzezinski, "shows how important nuances can be. While the Soviets should share 'a substantial common interest' with us, I felt that recent Soviet behavior demonstrated that such a common interest did not yet exist, and that we should make it clear to the Soviet leaders that their actions were not consistent with the notion of a stable and increasingly cooperative relationship."

Carter spent the last days before the summit in Washington with Brzezinski and the rest of the National Security Council, had lunch with German Chancellor Helmut Schmidt (who knew Brezhnev well), and conferred with Nixon over the telephone. Gerald Ford stopped by the White House with the advice that if Brezhnev started shouting the way he had in Vladivostok, Carter should be polite but firm. Admiral Stansfield Turner, the head of the CIA, showed the president videotape of Brezhnev's meetings with Nixon and Ford so that Carter could familiarize himself with the Soviet leader's mannerisms.

Jimmy, Rosalynn, and Amy Carter took a helicopter from the White House to Andrews Air Force Base. Eight hours later they landed in Vienna. Carter drove straight from the airport to the United States ambassador's residence, a three-story villa erected in the early 1930s for coal baron Karl Brod, who fled the Nazis and came to America in 1938. Brezhnev flew in early the next morning in a blue-and-white Ilyushin 62, wearing a dark-blue suit hung with medals including four Orders of Lenin. Only afterward did the 78-page SALT II arrive in Vienna. The negotiating marathon lasted until two o'clock in the morning before the summit, but the documents could not be delivered to Vienna for another day because the Soviets had nothing better in Geneva than an old typewriter, stiff paper, and a fifties-vintage photocopier. When the typist made a mistake, she had to retype the whole page from the start.

The highest-ranking CIA representative on the negotiating team presented his KGB counterpart with a t-shirt reading "Free the Tyuratam Eighteen." This was an inside joke that only those initiated into the mysteries of disarmament could understand. It referred to eighteen heavy missile launchers that the Soviets had located at a proving range in Kazakhstan and had not included in the strategic arms totals because they were "launchers for testing only." The Americans regarded this as a childish ruse, and only at the last minute, in a conciliatory gesture, did Moscow agree to dismantle a dozen of these launchers while promising to designate the others accurately and include them in the calculation.

Vienna was burbling with excitement. The last summit between superpower leaders that the Austrian capital hosted was between Kennedy and Khrushchev in 1961. Life-size figures of Brezhnev and Carter made of papier-mâché and marzipan appeared in the window of Der Demel sweet shop, playing chess with marzipan rockets.

The original schedule was changed so that both leaders could enjoy a warm, lovely day. Carter took a day trip out of town with his wife and daughter, while Brezhnev had a sightseeing trip through Vienna and a tour of Schönbrunn palace, once the Habsburg summer residence. At one point, he got out of his car to lay a wreath at the Soviet war memorial that the Viennese call "the grave of the unknown looter."

Then came the first meeting at the Hofburg. Carter strode briskly up the long steps and entered the gilded salons energetically. Five minutes passed before Brezhnev emerged sluggishly and heavily from the elevator. Arm in arm, they walked to the richly ornamented sixteenth-century reception hall where they chatted in the same chairs that John F. Kennedy and Nikita Khrushchev had sat in eighteen years earlier. When the press photographers called for a handshake, Brezhnev gripped Carter's hand firmly. They exchanged broad smiles. The 1979 Vienna summit was off to an affable start. The day ended with the gala at the Opera.

Discussions began the following day at the United States embassy. Brezhnev read his text from a script. While Carter spoke, he glanced from time to time at his handwritten notes on a yellow pad. That was where he jotted down something Brezhnev said to him the previous day, taking him mildly by surprise: "God will not forgive us if we fail." Gromyko reacted immediately to this word, raising a finger in the direction of the ceiling and saying, "You know, the guy upstairs." Later, the Soviet delegation spokesman attempted to replace the word "God" with "future generations," but Carter wrote down what he heard.

They paused to have lunch and allow Brezhnev time for a nap. Then they talked for two more hours. Brezhnev seemed to be in better shape than the Americans expected. He chided them time and again for their sins —plans for building the MX missile, which was mobile, irked him particularly. "I can't understand why you're building it." He warned that the fact it was mobile made it unverifiable, which put further negotiations at risk. Carter educated him about the fact that it could be tracked and verified in the same way as a stationary launcher, and thus fell within the negotiated settlement. On several occasions Brezhnev made as if to leave the table, but the atmosphere was generally good despite the bluffing. At one point he said, "We think that everyone is in favor of detente and good relations with the exception of certain persons." Smiling, he pointed at Secretary Vance, who was on especially good terms with the Russians. Everyone at the table chuckled; they knew whom Brezhnev had in mind. Brzezinski, regarded in both Moscow and Washington as a hawk who was particularly unyielding in relation with the Kremlin, pointed at himself and they all laughed out loud.

Over supper at the American ambassador's residence that same evening, as the vodka flowed, Brezhnev recounted with verve his hunting exploits in Siberia and Georgia. He boasted of what a good shot he was, and the rest of the Soviet delegation nodded energetically along.

— ★ —

The one planned occasion for longer private talks was an hour-long conversation accompanied only by the interpreters. For the Kremlin, the very fact of equal treatment had enormous symbolic import. For this reason the Soviets wanted Brezhnev and Carter to spend as much time as possible with each other.

"When Carter met alone with Brezhnev, Brezhnev—as Carter later told me—seemed unable to cope with a direct and informal discussion," Brzezinski recalled. "His translator had a file next to him, with different topics indexed, and he would reach into the file, pull out an appropriate piece of paper, and Brezhnev would read his response to Carter's comments from the piece of paper."

Finally came the moment they had all been waiting for. Twelve hundred reporters and hundreds of press photographers and television crews managed to crowd into the Redoutensaal, the white-and-gold dance and concert hall of the Hofburg. In that same palace where the Congress of Vienna had gone on for almost a year, Carter and Brezhnev, attended by their closest staff, signed SALT II, the Strategic Arms Limitation Agreement, at one o'clock in the afternoon. In the photo later seen around the world and featured in all the diplomatic chronicles, Zbigniew Brzezinski stands behind Carter and Andrey Gromyko stands behind Brezhnev. Gromyko wears his usual grumpy expression, while Brzezinski smiles as broadly as if he were posing for a wedding photo.

"I returned to Washington from Vienna feeling fairly satisfied," wrote Brzezinski in his *Memoirs*. "The meeting had been sober, without the excessive effusiveness which I feared might mislead the American public, which tends to oscillate from euphoria over détente to hysteria over the Cold War. The SALT agreement itself, I always believed and continue to believe, was in the American interest, for it imposed stricter limits on the Soviet side at the time when it had genuine momentum in its military buildup."

The ratification process quickly ran into trouble. The Soviet aggression against Afghanistan was the final nail in the coffin.

In April 1979, two months before the Vienna summit, the Americans met with opponents to the pro-Moscow Afghan government to find out what they needed. Earlier, the CIA had begun training mujahideen in Pakistan and broadcasting radio programs into Afghanistan. On July 3, two weeks after the Vienna ceremony and on the eve of Independence Day, President Carter signed the first directive on the subject of covert aid for opponents of the pro-communist regime in Kabul. Brzezinski admitted many years later that "On that day I wrote a note to the president in which I explained my view that this aid would evoke a Soviet military intervention. We did not force the Russians into intervention, but we deliberately increased its probability."

Brzezinski's contact with the ideological enemy had taken him to Vienna far earlier. Exactly twenty years before he stood behind Carter and smiled to the cameras, he was in Vienna for the World Festival of Youth and Students.

Carefully staged festivals were an important element in communist campaign to capture hearts and minds of a young generation. The Vienna Festival was the first to be held outside the communist bloc. The previous one, held in Moscow in 1957, had as its motto "For Peace and Friendship." The motto selected for the one in Vienna was "For Peace and Friendship and Peaceful Coexistence." The fact that the Festival's planning was supervised personally by Alexander Shelepin, the new head of the KGB, and the former head the World Federation of Democratic

Youth, was some measure of the importance it was accorded in Moscow.

The American National Student Association decided to boycott the festival in Vienna, but the CIA nevertheless wanted to make sure that anti-communist students from America were present at the event. It made use of a small operational unit especially created for this purpose under the name Independent Service for Information (ISI). The names of several of those involved in the Vienna effort would later become well known. The head and main organizer of the Vienna excursion was Gloria Steinem, then fresh from a student exchange in India and looking for a job. The ISI offered her a hundred dollars a week and an office not far from Harvard. She prepared propaganda material for young Americans who decided to go to Vienna and also selected a small group whose reservations were made and paid for by the ISI, or in practice by the CIA. The star of this group was a young Harvard academic, Zbigniew Brzezinski. In Vienna he went around deliberately jostling Soviet delegates and trying to entice them into political debates. During the Festival's closing ceremonies, Brzezinski and one of his fellow operatives, a journalist Walter Pincus, concealed themselves on the roof of a building overlooking the Vienna Rathausplatz, and, after getting across from one roof to another, separated by a 7-story drop between the two buildings, unfurled Algerian and Hungarian flags with their central symbols cut out as a sign of solidarity with the nations of the Third World and the struggle for freedom in the communist bloc, as well as a banner reading "Peace and Freedom" in German.

# Notes

Brzezinski's approach to the Soviet question, Z. Brzezinski, *Power and Principle. Memoirs of the National Security Advisor 1977–1981*, pp. 340–344.

The Vienna Summit, Z. Brzezinski, *Power and Principle. Memoirs of the National Security Advisor 1977–1981*, pp. 149–150.

Vienna 1959, Hugh Wilford, *The Mighty Wurlitzer. How the CIA Played America*, pp. 141–144.

# THE AFGHAN TRAP

Every politician probably has a photograph in his archives that was unexpectedly used against him, as well as an interview that caused him trouble while making his opponents gloat. In Zbig's case both the photo and the interview are connected with Afghanistan.

First, the photo. Original caption: "Khyber Pass, Pakistan: United States Security Adviser Zbigniew Brzezinski looks into Afghanistan through the sights of a machine gun at a Pakistan Army outpost here on the border 2/3. Brzezinski toured the area and then continued talks with the Pakistan delegation in regards to an aid package."

"While in Pakistan," recollects Brzezinski, "Christopher [Warren Christopher—Deputy Secretary of State] and I paid a visit to Afghan refugee camps, where we were saturated with very emotional and moving appeals for American arms. Separately, I paid a visit to a Pakistani military outpost in the Khyber Pass, where the commanding officer showed me a Chinese version of the Soviet automatic AK-47 rifle. As requested, I inspected the weapon (muzzle downward) and returned it to the Pakistanis, declining the suggestion that I fire it. On my return to Washington, I was amazed to find that a great furor had developed over the picture of me with the rifle in my hands. According to some press reports, I had aimed the weapon at Afghanistan, others had me firing it. Those who particularly resented my role in shaping our response to the Soviet actions in the region and who would like to see the United States conduct its foreign policy purely through a display of good intentions seized on this picture as symbolic of my "hawkishness"—while I saw in that emotional reaction a symptom of the malaise besetting some American liberals."

Writing his memoirs in 1983, Zbig could never have imagined that the photo from the Khyber Pass would take on a life of its own almost twenty years later. It began bouncing around the internet on a massive scale after September 11, 2001, and it is still in circulation today along with the information that the Pakistani soldier next to Brzeziński is none other than Osama bin Laden. The caption reads "Zbigniew Brzezinski visiting 'his boy,' Osama Bin Laden, in training with the Pakistan Army, 1981" or "here's some photos of the Trilateral co-founder with his favorite terrorist." It was enough that the soldier had a beard. The fact that he was at least four inches shorter than bin Laden didn't matter.

The interview was a more serious problem, hard to laugh off.

Interview with Zbigniew Brzezinski, Le Nouvel Observateur (France), Jan 15-21, 1998, p. 76

*Q: The former director of the CIA, Robert Gates, stated in his memoirs ["From the Shadows"], that American intelligence services began to aid the Mujahadeen in Afghanistan 6 months before the Soviet intervention. In this period you were the national security adviser to President Carter. You therefore played a role in this affair. Is that correct?*

*Brzezinski: Yes. According to the official version of history, CIA aid to the Mujahadeen began during 1980, that is to say, after the Soviet army invaded Afghanistan, 24 Dec 1979. But the reality, secretly guarded until now, is completely otherwise: Indeed, it was July 3, 1979 that President Carter signed the first directive for secret aid to the opponents of the pro-Soviet regime* in Kabul. And that very day, I wrote a note to the president in which I explained to him that in my opinion this aid was going to induce a Soviet military intervention.

Q: Despite this risk, you were an advocate of this covert action. But perhaps you yourself desired this Soviet entry into war and looked to provoke it?

Brzezinski: It isn't quite that. We didn't push the Russians to intervene, but we knowingly increased the probability that they would.

Q: When the Soviets justified their intervention by asserting that they intended to fight against a secret involvement of the United States in Afghanistan, people didn't believe them. However, there was a basis of truth. You don't regret anything today?

Brzezinski: Regret what? That secret operation was an excellent idea. It had the effect of drawing the Russians into the Afghan trap and you want me to regret it? The day that the Soviets officially crossed the border, I wrote to President Carter: We now have the opportunity of giving to the USSR its Vietnam war. Indeed, for almost 10 years, Moscow had to carry on a war unsupportable by the government, a conflict that brought about the demoralization and finally the breakup of the Soviet empire.

Q: And neither do you regret having supported the Islamic [integrisme], having given arms and advice to future terrorists?

Brzezinski: What is most important to the history of the world? The Taliban, or the collapse of the Soviet empire? Some stirred-up Moslems or the liberation of Central Europe and the end of the cold war?

Q: Some stirred-up Moslems? But it has been said and repeated: Islamic fundamentalism represents a world menace today.

> *Brzezinski: Nonsense! It is said that the West had a global policy in regard to Islam. That is stupid. There isn't a global Islam. Look at Islam in a rational manner and without demagoguery or emotion. It is the leading religion of the world with 1.5 billion followers. But what is there in common among Saudi Arabian fundamentalism, moderate Morocco, Pakistan militarism, Egyptian pro-Western or Central Asian secularism? Nothing more than what unites the Christian countries.*

So *Le Nouvel Observateur* had it. Later, Zbig said many times, and repeated to me, that he had not signed off on the interview despite a provision in the contract giving him a chance to do so, and that his remarks were out of context.

Instead of trying to figure out whether the interviewer was wrong, or Brzezinski got carried away, or that we are dealing with a chain of mistakes and awkwardness, let's look at the facts.

Moscow was interfering increasingly actively in Afghan affairs, and although one part of the CIA was perfectly aware of this, a different part was so blind that it was considering Afghanistan as the site for an observation station to replace one in Iran that America had lost when Khomeini took power.

In April 1979, the Americans met with opponents to the pro-Moscow Afghan government to find out what they needed. Earlier, the CIA had begun training mujahedeen in Pakistan and broadcasting into Afghanistan. Carter's July 3, 1979 directive on covert aid to opponents of the pro-communist regime in Kabul was modest in scale and did not envision the supply of arms.

On September 11, Afghan president Nur Mohammed Taraki held consultations in Moscow on candidates to replace Prime Minister Hafizullah Amin, suspected of colluding with the CIA. Two days later, Amin beat Taraki to the punch, murdering him, announcing his resignation, and accepting a congratulatory telegram from Moscow. On December 23, the KGB transported its agent Babrak Karmal, a communist, to Kabul. Karmal had been exiled to Prague as Afghan ambassador a few months earlier. On Christmas Eve 1979, Soviet troops poured in. A special KGB unit disguised in Afghan uniforms stormed the presidential palace and shot Amin on December 26. Two days later, Karmal was named general secretary of the party, chairman of the Afghan Revolutionary Council, prime minister, and commander-in-chief of the armed forces. The politburo session that made these decisions was held under KGB supervision at Bagram air base. Officially, Karmal proclaimed that he stood at the head of a "popular uprising" against "the Amin tyranny."

When the Soviets invaded Afghanistan, President Carter was shocked.

Did Brzezinski provoke Moscow? It seems unlikely that he wanted Moscow to intervene, because he had issued so many personal warnings and prevailed on the State Department to caution the Kremlin. It didn't take a genius to foresee that Soviet intervention would be a fatal blow to SALT II, the ratification of which was so important to the Carter team.

What does Brzezinski himself say about Afghanistan in his memoirs? We should remember that they came out in 1983, eighteen years before America heard of bin Laden and many years before cooperation with Islamic fundamentalists was viewed as blameworthy. In other words, Brzezinski could have safely blown his own horn in 1983 about how cunningly he had used Arab extremists in the fight against Moscow. But he didn't.

"I monitored with mounting apprehension the intensifying Soviet military involvement in Afghanistan and I pressed for a stronger US reaction. . . . My notes show, for instance, that I brought this issue up several times in late March and early April, and that in early May 1979 I warned the President that the Soviets would be in a position, if them came to dominate Afghanistan, to promote a separate Baluchistan, which would give them access to the Indian Ocean while dismembering Pakistan and Iran. . . . By mid-summer we had received numerous intelligence reports of widespread resistance throughout Afghanistan to the Soviet-supported regime, but the Soviets rebuffed all our warnings that their growing intrusion would jeopardize the American-Soviet relationship. On the President's orders we began to publicize our concerns, in order to give greater credibility to our private admonitions. . . . with the President's approval, I gave a public speech, which the *New York Times* reported (August 3) prominently on page 1 under the headline "U.S. is Indirectly Pressing Russians to Halt Afghanistan Intervention."

On March 28, 1980—three months after the Soviet invasion of Afghanistan—Zbig wrote in the NSC Weekly Report #134, his regular report to the president, that there were two contradictory interpretations of the operation and wondered whether the invasion was an aberration, diverging from normal Soviet conduct, or a symptom.

## Aberration

Those who see it as an aberration tend to feel that the primary motive for the Soviet actions was defensive, that the Soviets do not have longer-term regional ambitions beyond Afghanistan, and that they are likely to consider seriously some mutually acceptable formula for a solution to the problem generated by their invasion of Afghanistan. Proponents of this school of thought do not deny that the Soviet Union occasionally acts aggressively, but see that largely as an expedient reaction to opportunities rather than as a manifestation of a more sustained trend. Because of that, one is entitled to nurture hopes of a relatively early return to more normal East-West relations, including genuine progress on some of the more important bilateral US-Soviet issues.

# ZBIG

## Symptom

Those who argue otherwise feel that the Soviet Union is currently in an assertive phase of its history, with the acquisition of military power giving its foreign policy both greater scope and more frequent temptations to use its power to advance policy goals. Soviet behavior is still prudent, but it does involve a gradual shift from political encouragement of often geographically remote ideological sympathizers, to more direct support of them through the use of Cuban proxies in the mid-'70s, to even more direct projection of Soviet military power itself currently. In other words, Soviet behavior is symptomatic of a long-term historical drive, with military power supplanting Marxist ideology as its basic dynamic source.

As you probably anticipate, I lean to the second school of thought. I would also argue additionally that there are certain constants in Soviet foreign policy, and the drive toward the Persian Gulf is one of them. I am struck by the fact that the draft agreement between the Soviet Union and Nazi German, which was being negotiated secretly between Molotov and Ribbentrop in 1940, including the following passage: "The Soviet Union declares that its territorial aspirations center south of the national territory of the Soviet Union in the direction of the Indian Ocean." Moreover, the German Ambassador reported on November 25, 1940, that Molotov told him that the Soviet Union would associate itself with the Axis powers, "provided that the area south of Batumi and Baku in the general direction of the Persian Gulf is recognized as the center of the aspirations of the Soviet Union."

The argument between those who think that Afghanistan is an aberration and those who think it is a symptom is not merely an intellectual exercise. Though we are all in agreement with what needed to be done, I suspect that there potential differences among us about the future (and these differences could complicate planning for the NATO Summit): how long should the present policy be maintained; to what extent should the Allies be pressed to recognize the wider and strategic character of the Soviet challenge; how energetically should we try to reinforce the Western presence in the Persian Gulf/Indian Ocean area; how important is it to beef up Pakistan; what is the strategic urgency of moving more rapidly on the Palestinian problem; and, finally, how fruitful are likely to be any early efforts to improve relations with the Soviet Union?

On that last point, my view is that in a quiet but persistent way we need to replicate in this new third central strategic zone (southwest Asia) what we have done earlier in Western Europe and the Far East; create a sense of security, and halt Soviet expansionism. Once our efforts are credible, I think we have a very good chance to return to détente and to seek the humane and morally imperative goals with which I hope history will identify you."

In a 1996 book, Robert Gates states that Pakistan had been pressuring the United States for years to arm the insurgents, but Carter refused in the hope of finding diplomatic methods of avoiding war.

No one could have been in a position at the time to envision the enormous extent to which it would contribute to the fall of the communist superpower. On January 20, 1980, immediately after Carter's first public announcement of sanctions and approval of arms supplies to the mujahedeen, Anatoli Dobrynin, the long-serving Soviet ambassador in America, warned Brezhnev, as he later recalled, "Watch out for Carter. He is behaving like a bull in a China shop." Brezhnev responded: "Don't worry. It will be over in three to four weeks."

Operation Cyclone, the program to train, arm, and finance the Afghan mujahedeen who fought the Soviets until 1989, became over time a symbol of the most controversial effort that the CIA ever undertook. Beginning with a modest $20-30 million in 1980, it grew to $630 million in 1987. However, it was not its cost that made it notorious, or even its final success. What makes the operation explosive is the question of who benefited from the aid and the degree to which the roots of Islamic terrorism lie in the mujahedeen war financed to a large degree by the American taxpayer. Does Zbigniew Brzezinski deserve the title that began at a certain moment to be applied to him: "The godfather of al-Qaeda"?

In an interview with *Real News* on January 15, 2010, Brzezinski said

"They would have continued fighting without our help, because they were also getting a lot of money from the Persian Gulf and the Arab states, and they weren't going to quit. They didn't decide to fight because we urged them to. They're fighters, and they prefer to be independent. They just happen to have a curious complex: they don't like foreigners with guns in their country. And they were going to fight the Soviets. But giving them Stingers was a very important forward step in defeating the Soviets, and that's all to the good as far as I'm concerned."

In February 1980, a month after the invasion, Brzezinski met face to face in Pakistan with that country's president, Mohammed Zia, to discuss the clandestine operation. From there, he flew to Saudi Arabia where he received assurances that the kingdom would match America's aid to the mujahedeen. "The purpose of coordinating with the Pakistanis would be to make the Soviets bleed for as much and as long as is possible." Brzezinski was clear on his intentions.

"We started providing weapons to the Mujahedin, from various sources again—for example, some Soviet arms from the Egyptians and the Chinese. We even got Soviet arms from the Czechoslovak Communist government, since it was obviously susceptible to material incentives; and at some point we started buying arms for the Mujahedin from the Soviet army in Afghanistan, because that army was increasingly corrupt," Brzezinski said on CNN.

President Zia, who feared a strong Soviet presence next door and saw Afghanistan's ally India in the traditional way—as a mortal enemy—not only had no objections to the operation but also wanted to play an active part. We will never know whether it was more a matter of diverting some of the money to other ends or of deciding who would get how much and when. Inter-Service Intelligence (ISI), the Pakistani military intelligence agency, became the coordinator of the whole undertaking. It turned out that, as it divided the funding, the ISI favored pro-Pakistani Islamists above all. The "Afghan Arabs" usually fought alongside this faction, which is surely the origin of the theory that they were really the ones the CIA supported.

In his book *Unholy Wars*, John K. Cooley writes about the rules laid down in Brzezinski's January 1980 meeting with Zia in Islamabad: "Zia placed three absolute conditions for allowing shipment of the arms from Egypt, China and other points of origin, including the United States, through Pakistan to the holy warriors fighting the Russians. First, the countries concerned—the US, Egypt, Saudi Arabia, China and eventually Britain, France and even Israel, were to maintain absolute silence about the shipments. They would deny that they took place at all, repeatedly and whenever necessary. Second, arms and other war supplies were to be shipped to Pakistan by the fastest available means (hence the early airlifts from US "facilities" in Sadat's Egypt, where Sadat's full cooperation and commitment made possible both speed and secrecy, initially at least). Third, the shipments by air (as opposed to overland shipment from China and Iran, and the great bulk of shipments which came by sea to Karachi and other Pakistani ports), were to be limited to two planeloads per week."

The American Stinger missiles allowed the partisans to defend themselves against Soviet helicopters. Yet this portable air-ground missile, which made its debut on the British side during the 1982 Falklands war, did not appear in Afghanistan until the fall of 1986. The mujahedeen shot down about a hundred Soviet aircraft and, most importantly, broke the absolute Soviet control of the air and made it harder to carry out airborne operations. The Stingers proved so effective that the United States bought up the unused ones in the nineties to prevent them falling into the hands of anti-American terrorists. This program was covertly resumed after the American intervention in Afghanistan in late 2001.

The Americans favored the Afghan forces led by Ahmen Dhah Massoud, a Kabul ex-student who was 26 when the Soviets invaded. His valor earned him the name "Lion of Panjshir." A devout Muslim, he always carried a book by the Sufi mystic Ghazali, regarded by historians as the most important Muslim after the prophet Muhammad. Massoud categorically rejected the interpretation of Islam followed by the Taliban and Al Qaeda. Following the withdrawal of Soviet troops from Afghanistan, the Wall Street Journal named Massoud "the Afghan who won the Cold War." In 1992, he returned to the role of an armed opposition leader and became the leader of the Northern Alliance, made up mostly of Afghan Tajiks and Uzbeks. On September 9, 2011, two days before the terrorist attack on America, Massoud was murdered by Al Qaeda.

The image of America nurturing bin Laden at its breast is sensational and sells well, but has little in common with reality.

The so-called Afghan Arabs were trained with Arab, not American money. Al Qaeda's number two, Ayman al-Zawahiri, confirmed that the "Afghan Arabs" did not receive any US funding during the war in Afghanistan. In the book that was described as his last will, "*Knights Under the Prophet's Banner,*" al-Zawahiri says the Afghan Arabs were funded with money from Arab sources, which amounted to hundreds of millions of dollars:

". . . The financing of the activities of the Arab mujahidin in Afghanistan came from aid sent to Afghanistan by popular organizations. It was substantial aid."

"The Arab mujahidin did not confine themselves to financing their own jihad but also carried Muslim donations to the Afghan mujahidin themselves. Usama Bin Ladin has apprised me of the size of the popular Arab support for the Afghan mujahidin that amounted, according to his sources, to $200 million in the form of military aid alone in 10 years. Imagine how much aid was sent by popular Arab organizations in the non-military fields such as medicine and health, education and vocational training, food, and social assistance...."

"Through the unofficial popular support, the Arab mujahidin established training centers and centers for the call to the faith. They formed fronts that trained and equipped thousands of Arab mujahidin and provided them with living expenses, housing, travel and organization."

The Afghans liked Arab money but did not look favorably on Arabs filled with zeal to convert them to the purest variety of Islam.

Abdullah Anas, an Algerian who was one of the foremost Afghan Arab organizers has also confirmed that the CIA had no relationship with the Afghan Arabs. Speaking on the French television program *Zone Interdit* on September 12, 2004, Anas stated:

"If you say there was a relationship in the sense that the CIA used to meet with Arabs, discuss with them, prepare plans with them, and to fight with them—it never happened."

Freelance cameraman Peter Jouvenal recounts the piquant way an Afghan described relations with the Arab comrades-in-arms: "Whenever we had a problem with them, we just killed them. They thought they were kings."

Brzezinski states that September 11 did not change his assessment of the secret aid to the Afghan partisans. He agrees with the view that America's biggest mistake was leaving Afghanistan to its own unhappy fate the moment the Soviets withdrew. He also feels that the problem of terrorism would be even more serious if the Soviet Union still existed, because it would support its terrorist pawns among the Palestinians, Syrians, Libyans, and so on.

— ★ —

## ZBIG

In his 1995 book *In Confidence*, Anatoly Dobrynin calls the invasion of Afghanistan a great mistake.

During a Politburo session on November 13, 1986, Marshal Sergey Akhromeyev, chief of the general staff of the armed forces, said that

"[t]here is no single piece of land in this country which as not been occupied by a Soviet soldier. Nevertheless, the majority of the territory remains in the hands of rebels. . . . We control Kabul and the provincial centers, but on occupied territory we cannot establish authority. We have lost the battle for the Afghan people. The government is supported by a minority of the population. Our army has fought for five years. It is now in a position to maintain the situation on the level that exists now. But under such conditions the war will continue for a long time." (National Security Archive, made public on February 14, 2009, just before the twentieth anniversary of the last Soviet units from Afghanistan.)

On May 10, 1988, the central committee of the Soviet communist party approved a "confidential" letter to party members on Afghanistan.

> *One has to admit that essentially we put our bets on the military solution, on suppressing the counterrevolution with force. We did not even fully use the existing opportunities for neutralization of the hostile attitudes of the local population towards us. We have to assess critically some aspects of functioning of our adviser apparatus in Afghanistan as well. It did many things to provide assistance in strengthening the PDPA and the people's regime. However, often our people, acting out of their best intentions, tried to transplant the approached we are accustomed to onto the Afghan soil, encouraged the Afghans to copy our ways. All this did not help our cause; it bred the feelings of dependency on the part of the Afghan leaders in regard to the Soviet Union both*

> *in the sphere of military operations and in the economic sphere. . . .*
>
> *By the beginning of May 1988, we lost 13,310 people [dead] in Afghanistan; 35,478 Soviet officers and soldiers were wounded, many of whom became disabled; 301 people are missing in action. . . . The Afghan losses, naturally, were much heavier [than ours], including the losses among the civilian population.*
>
> *One should not disregard the economic factor either. If the enemy in Afghanistan received weapons and ammunition for hundreds of millions and later even billions of dollars, the Soviet-Afghan side also had to shoulder adequate expenditures. The war in Afghanistan costs us 5 billion rubles a year.*

At the 1987 year-end lunch in New York, Robert Gates, then Deputy DCI (Director of Central Intelligence), bet Michael Armacost, Undersecretary of State for Political Affairs, twenty-five dollars the Soviets would not be out of Afghanistan before the end of Reagan's term.

For Gorbachev ending the war in Afghanistan, which he characterized as "a bleeding wound," was a priority from the moment he assumed power in 1985. The Politburo made the decision on October 17, 1985. The timetable for withdrawing the troops was not ready until the fall of 1987, and Gorbachev announced the decision on February 8, 1988.

On February 15, 1989, the commander of the Soviet contingent in Afghanistan, General Boris Gromov, was the last soldier of the occupying army to cross the bridge on the Amu Darya, thus ending a war that had gone on for almost ten years.

Gates wrote in his memoirs:

> *"The Chinese had a saying about the Soviet appetite for territory and their unwillingness to give it up: 'What the*

*bear has eaten, he never spits out.' Well, needless to say, I was wrong. Months later I paid Mike Armacost the twenty-five dollars—the best money I ever spent. I also told myself it would be the last time I'd make intelligence forecast based on a fortune cookie wisdom."*

Afghanistan always made Brzezinski uneasy. Over the winter of 2009 I discussed it with him several times. He told me that when American special forces drove the Taliban out of Kabul with unexpected ease, he telephoned Rumsfeld and advised him, "Don, proclaim victory and come home."

## Notes

The Khyber Pass photo: *Power and Principle*, p. 449.

Dobrynin's warning: John K. Cooley, *Unholy Wars*, pp. 18–19.

Al-Zawahiri quote: Al-Sharq al-Awsat, December 3, 2001, Foreign Broadcast Information Service.

Jouvenal anecdote: Peter Bergen, *Holy War Inc.*

Communist party "confidential letter": The National Security Archives. Alexander Lyakhovsky, *Tragedy and Valor of Afghan*, Iskon, Moscow 1995.

"The Chinese had a saying . . . ": Gates, *From the Shadows*, p. 431.

# BRANDED

In July 1976 Brzezinski was at Shabbat dinner at the home of Shimon Peres, the Israeli defense minister, when plans were ready for the rescue operation at Entebbe. Brzezinski surprised his hosts by throwing a direct question at Peres: 'Why don't you send the IDF to rescue the hostages at Entebbe?" The Defense Minister started explaining the reasons against such an operation. Brzezinski was not convinced. 24 hours later Israeli commandos landed at Entebbe airport outside Kampala, the capital of Uganda, after traveling four thousand miles. They freed 103 hostages who had been passengers on an Air France plane hijacked by Palestinian terrorists on June 27. Five commandos were wounded. The only one to perish was the mission commander, 30-year-old Jonathan Netanyahu, the elder brother of today's prime minister. All the hijackers, 3 hostages, and 45 Ugandan soldiers paid with their lives. The commandos destroyed eleven MiG-17s belonging to the Ugandan air force.

Brzezinski was a private individual at the time, although he was the main adviser to a serious candidate for the White House. He was received in Israel with honors. "Probably contrary to the expectations of my Israeli hosts," he wrote later, "my trip to the Golan Heights and my travels within the country convinced me of the futility of seeking security through the acquisition of territory. It became clear to me that Israel could never acquire enough territory to compensate for Arab hostility."

He has never changed his mind.

After the fall of communism, no subject has provoked Brzezinski to such frequent public statements, usually controversial, as Israeli policy. One obsession—"conquer the Kremlin"—has been replaced by another—"solve the Middle East conflict." On various occasions, he has uttered things no other politician would dare to say.

In the summer of 2009 there was unrelenting speculation about who would restrain Teheran's nuclear ambitions—and when, and how. Neoconservatives were saying and writing that, as long as the Iranian nuclear threat remained in place, it was necessary to reckon with the possibility of an Israeli attack on Iran. John Bolton, George W. Bush's assistant secretary of state and later ambassador to the UN, regretted that Israel had not taken action before the end of Bush's term because Obama opposed an attack and looked less favorably on Israel's hard line.

On September 20, 2009, Brzezinski, in an interview with The Daily Beast, suggested President Obama should make it clear to the Israelis that if they attempted to attack Iran's nuclear weapons sites the US Air Force would stop them.

"We are not exactly impotent little babies," Brzezinski said. "They have to fly over our airspace in Iraq. Are we just going to sit there and watch? . . . We have to be serious about denying them that right. That means a denial where you aren't just saying it. If they fly over, you go up and confront them. They have the choice of turning back or not. No one wishes for this but it could be a 'Liberty' in reverse." (The USS Liberty was a US Navy technical research ship that the Israeli Air Force mistakenly attacked during the Six Day War in 1967.)

Much earlier, when speculation began that Brzezinski would be an advisor to candidate Obama, the first sharply critical reaction came from parts of the American Jewish community.

"Brzezinski is not an adviser to the campaign," former Ambassador Dennis Ross, then a senior adviser on Middle East affairs to the Obama campaign, said at the time. "There is a lot of disinformation that is being pushed, but he is not an adviser to the campaign. Brzezinski came out and supported Obama early because of the war in Iraq. A year or so ago they talked a couple of times. That's the extent of it, and Sen. Obama has made it clear that on other Middle Eastern issues, Brzezinski is not who he looks to. They don't have the same views."

In Washington, Brzezinski had long ago been tagged as an "enemy of Israel." That is not an easy label to shed. Especially since Zbig himself, while regarding it as unjustified and even a symptom of paranoia, does nothing to resist it. Obviously, he is not particularly interested in proving the negative.

The accusation did not come out of nowhere. For more than thirty years Brzezinski has stubbornly maintained, probably more frequently than anyone who means anything in Washington, that the unresolved Middle East conflict threatens America's interests while also endangering Israel's security, and that no small part of the blame lies in Israel's shortsighted policies. Because he talks and writes about these things passionately, and doesn't mince his words, the mutual prejudices have piled up. The government of Israel can sound like a broken record, and so can Zbig.

A good part of the hostility toward the United States in the Muslim world results from viewing America as the guardian of Israel's interests—and a misconceived version of those interests to boot. The Palestinians, Brzezinski says, are too divided and too weak, and Israel too divided and too strong, to be pushed in the direction of lasting peace. The United States alone can play such a role, but refuses to do so. Obama should be more decisive and insist on the one realistic road to peace, as difficult as it is. The basic principles are, first, the renunciation by the Palestinians of the right to return to the territory of today's Israel—after all, it would be hard to demand that Israel should commit suicide in the name of peace. Second, an authentic division of Jerusalem, with the western part of the city as capital of the Jewish state, the eastern part as capital of the Palestinian state, and the Old City shared under some form of international supervision. Third, the 1967 borders with some territorial swaps, the Palestinians receiving compensation elsewhere in exchange for major Israeli settlements created during the occupation. Fourth, American or NATO troops deployed along the Jordan, to ensure Israeli security when a demilitarized Palestinian state arises.

Such a position leads to charges that Zbig is attempting to impose his solutions on the parties to the conflict. Dennis Ross, the main Middle East negotiator under George H. W. Bush and Bill Clinton, is critical:

"If the myth of [George W.] Bush and the neoconservatives was to believe in our capacity to impose our form of democracy and our image of what the region should be, the myth of many on the left and self-described 'realists' like Zbigniew Brzezinski may be that we can impose peace between Israelis and Palestinians and transform the Middle East in the process."

"'Impose' means to force it down their throats," responds Brzezinski. "The word I use is 'help' because I don't think either side is prepared to make the concessions that are needed, and neither side is prepared to take the first step because it's always afraid that the other side will pocket the concessions."

Brzezinski feels that isolating Hamas only strengthens that organization, and that it would be better to talk. He answers the argument that Israel has only a single strong friend with the words: "The notion that we have to prove our friendship to Israel by starving the people of Gaza I just find immoral in content and not practical politically." He goes on to say in the discussion with Scowcroft and Ignatius that "[b]eyond that, there's a practical question. How long will Israel endure if we're driven out of the Middle East?"

"When I first went to the Middle East to push for Arab acquiescence to the Camp David peace treaty between Israel and Egypt, some of the Arabs said to me, 'You know, the crusaders were in Jerusalem for ninety years, and they are gone. We're not in a rush.' So there is legitimacy to Israeli concerns. But they have to ask themselves, 'Is that horrible scenario more likely or less likely if there's no peace?'"

In any case, the government of Israel rejects the kind of architecture propounded by Brzezinski and reiterated by Obama. The Palestinians themselves have not reacted to Zbig's idea—why should they renounce an army if they deserve an independent state? Would Brzezinski soften his criticism of Israel if Jews approved his idea and Arabs rejected it? He believes not only that the kind of peace he sketches out is possible, but also that its realization—reconciliation—could make Israel and Palestine into the Singapore of the Middle East.

"If I were an Israeli I would look at Dubai and Qatar and say to myself, Don't I want a piece of that? Once there is peace, the intelligence of the Israelis and Palestinians together could make them a dynamo for the region, financially and technologically," he says in his discussion with Scowcroft and Ignatius.

He notes that there will always be extremists ready to commit murder on both sides. "Are we supposed to let those people dominate the future?"

Here the past, not only of the Middle East but also of Zbig's position, rears its head. After the signing of the Camp David agreement—thanks mostly to Sadat, but also to Carter and, as Brzezinski openly admits, Cyrus Vance—Zbig did most of the talking at the press briefing. He mentioned that the agreement foresaw the presence of UN forces on the West Bank. That was the exact opposite of the Israeli position. "I do not know why Zbig said it," recalls Jim Hoagland, the State Department correspondent for the *Washington Post* at the time. "There was an uproar and a clarification was required. It's hard for me to believe that on an issue so vital to the whole agreement, Zbig didn't know that Begin wouldn't swallow it."

Jewish circles had already reacted unfavorably to Brzezinski's first personnel decisions. He entrusted Middle Eastern affairs to William Quandt, regarded as a reliable, credible expert. The director of AIPAC, the heart of the Israel lobby in America, and a senator intervened with Brzezinski over the nomination, describing Quandt as pro-Palestinian. This rumbled on for several months and it is precisely here that Brzezinski sees the source of the tension between himself and parts of the Jewish community. (It is worth noting that many years later Michael Oren, the historian and current ambassador of Israel in Washington, recognized Quandt's book on the Middle East conflict and American diplomacy as one of the best in the field.) Yet it seems debatable whether a single nomination could, in itself, produce so much mutual animosity.

Brzezinski surely won himself few fans in Israel for the way he characterized the main actors in the negotiations:

> *Sadat's personality stood in sharp contrast to that of Rabin. Warm, gracious, even ingratiating, he was at the same time poised and confident, and exuded the aura of a man willing to risk much—as in 1973—in order to win much.*

To that dollop of honey Brzezinski adds a dash of bitters by saying that the Egyptian president

> *also had a tendency to let himself be carried away by his own words, and I noted in my journal that 'my worry is that Sadat does not seem to differentiate clearly between fact and fiction, and I wonder how much of what he said was just for effect.'*

Brzezinski writes that Carter sometimes spoke of his willingness to lose the White House if that was the cost of true peace in the Middle East. "I think he was sincere," he comments. "Perhaps most importantly, Carter's feelings on Israel were always ambivalent. On the one hand, he felt that Israel was being intransigent; on the other, he genuinely did have an attachment to the country as 'the land of the Bible.'"

Relations with the Jewish community worsened to the degree the Carter team pressured the Israeli government. Brzezinski recalls that a good deal of the criticism was aimed at him, and allusions began to appear in the press.

> *I was presented as anti-Israeli, perhaps even worse than that, and the references to my Polish and Catholic background became increasingly pointed in some of the commentaries on the subject of the Middle East.*

Immediately after this, Zbig mentions that Begin invited him to breakfast at Blair House, where he was staying in Washington, and in the presence of reporters and TV crews handed him documents, discovered in the archives in Jerusalem, about how his father, Tadeusz Brzezinski, as a Polish diplomat in Germany, had been engaged in efforts to rescue Jews.

"I was deeply touched by this gesture of human sensitivity, especially since it came in the wake of some of the personal attacks on me and my role in seeking to promote a peaceful settlement in the Middle East. Begin and I then sat down to breakfast, and we talked about Jabotinsky's influence on him [Ze'ev Jabotinsky was a Zionist leader, author, and soldier, who in 1934 he wrote a draft constitution for the Jewish state which declared that the Arab minority would be on an equal footing with its Jewish counterpart "throughout all sectors of the country's public life.], about his vision of the future and the past. And I stressed to him that I was very impressed by the degree to which he lives the suffering of his people and yet is also the personification of the triumph of Israel. I suggested to Begin that the next stage is to make the triumph permanent through peaceful accommodation."

To my knowledge, Brzezinski never again took up this thread from his family history. However, he quite unexpectedly recalled it on December 11, 2010 during a long interview on Al Jazeera. Brzezinski was talking about what a big event the recovery of Polish independence in 1918 had been in his parents' lives. Then, with no particular pretext but rather out of a heartfelt need—although perhaps there was more to it than appeared—he told how, as a Polish diplomat in Germany, his father "was more involved in aiding Jews than was official Polish policy. He issued Polish passports to Polish Jews in Germany, and to German Jews."

He also recalls how, when Moscow released five dissidents including two Russian Jews in exchange for the freeing of some Soviet spies, Begin called him at home from Jerusalem to thank him for the *mitzvah*—a good deed deserving of gratitude.

Let us, however, leave Begin and the Carter-Brzezinski tandem behind and return to the early days of the flirtation, or perhaps rather the potential alliance, between Obama and Brzezinski.

Ardent adherents of Israel were particularly dismayed by the fact that Brzezinski came out in defense of the book by Stephen M. Walt of Harvard and John J. Mearsheimer of the University of Chicago on the power of the Israel lobby in America and its influence on foreign policy. The authors more or less stated that the political and material support that America provides for Israel does not serve the strategic interests of the United States. There is no moral rationale for this support, they argue, because even though Israel is a democracy, it is tainted by discrimination against its own Arab citizens and by the occupation. Since there are neither strategic nor moral reasons for the support, they ask, where does it come from? The answer, in their view, is simple: the power of the Israel lobby.

That lobby, they contend, has great influence on American foreign policy. Its core is the American Israel Public Affairs Committee (AIPAC).

Brzezinski has never spoken out on the controversial book. However, he looked favorably on earlier essays by its authors. In an article in *Foreign Policy* (July/August 2006), Brzezinski wrote:

"Given that the Middle East is currently the central challenge facing America, Professors John Mearsheimer and Stephen Walt have rendered a public service by initiating a much needed public debate on the role of the 'Israel lobby' in the shaping of US foreign policy."

Walt and Mearsheimer responded by thanking Brzezinski. For his part, Obama has distanced himself from their book.

On September 12, 2007, *Politico* quoted Alan Dershowitz of Harvard, regarded as Israel's most eloquent defender in the court of public opinion, as saying

"It is a tremendous mistake for Barack Obama to select as a foreign policy adviser the one person in public life who has chosen to support a bigoted book."

In an interview with *The Daily Telegraph* on May 27, 2008, Brzezinski vented his frustration and said of AIPAC that

> *They operate not by arguing but by slandering, vilifying, demonizing. They very promptly wheel out anti-Semitism. There is an element of paranoia in this inclination to view any serious attempt at a compromised peace as somehow directed against Israel.*

On March 11, 2009, the *New York Times* wrote that since Obama himself was greeted with a certain skepticism by certain pro-Israel groups during the presidential campaign, he is touchy on the subject and distanced himself at a certain moment from Zbigniew Brzezinski, who is sometimes critical of Israeli policy.

Before Netanyahu's visit in May 2011, Obama gave a speech at the State Department so controversial that several days later, as if in recompense, Congress accorded the Israeli prime minister a standing ovation. Brzezinski publicly opined after Obama's speech that the president had moved in the right direction, but not decisively enough.

On April 11, 2010, Brzezinski joined the late Rep. Stephen Solarz, an unbending defender of Israel's interests, in a call published in the *New York Times* for President Obama to make a bold journey to the Middle East.

"More than three decades ago, Israeli statesman Moshe Dayan, speaking about an Egyptian town that controlled Israel's only outlet to the Red Sea, declared that he would rather have Sharm el-Sheikh without peace than peace without Sharm el-Sheikh. Had his views prevailed, Israel and Egypt would still be in a state of war. Today, Prime Minister Binyamin Netanyahu, with his pronouncements about the eternal and undivided capital of Israel, is conveying an updated version of Dayan's credo—that he would rather have all of Jerusalem without peace than peace without all of Jerusalem."

To break the impasse, Brzezinski and Solarz wrote, announcing yet another American peace plan is not enough.

"Only a bold and dramatic gesture in a historically significant setting can generate the political and psychological momentum needed for a major breakthrough. Anwar Sadat's courageous journey to Jerusalem three decades ago accomplished just that, paving the way for the Camp David accords between Israel and Egypt."

"Similarly, President Obama should travel to the Knesset in Jerusalem and the Palestinian Legislative Council in Ramallah to call upon both sides to negotiate a final status agreement based on a specific framework for peace. He should do so in the company of Arab leaders and members of the Quartet, the diplomatic grouping of the United States, Russia, the European Union and the United Nations that is involved in the peace process. A subsequent speech by Obama in Jerusalem's Old City, addressed to all the people in the region and evocative of his Cairo speech to the Muslim world in June 2009, could be the culminating event in this journey for peace."

Today, the scenario for such a trip would be more complicated because the situation in the Middle East is more complex. Who should be invited from Egypt, Libya, Tunisia, Syria, or Yemen?

I asked the eminent Israeli political scientist and philosopher, Shlomo Avineri, about the charges against Brzezinski. A professor at the Hebrew University in Jerusalem, Avineri was director general of the Ministry of Foreign Affairs in Yitzhak Rabin's government from 1975 to 1977. In the spring of 1976, when it became clear that Carter had a chance of becoming president, Avineri visited Brzezinski in New York and invited him to Israel.

"Saying that Brzezinski is an anti-Semite is complete nonsense," said Avineri. He felt, though, that Brzezinski sees Israel exclusively in categories of American national interest—and in Brzezinski's perception there is nothing of the special empathy felt by the majority of American politicians. It is thus a coldly realistic perception. On the other hand, Avineri said, there is an element in Brzezinski of the Polish philo-Semitism characteristic of parts of the progressive Polish aristocracy. This is surely something he owes to his upbringing. It can be seen in the stance his father took when he attacked anti-Semitic goon squads with his cane. He probably did not like Begin because he saw in him an Israeli version of a prewar Polish National Democrat, an "Endek": ethnocentrism imbued with militarism and populism. Avineri also mentioned the role of Consul Brzezinski in Leipzig—his aid to Polish and German Jews without passports and the fact that Polish Jews in Leipzig contributed £50 to have the name of Tadeusz Brzezinski inscribed in the Golden Book of the National Fund in Jerusalem.

Avineri recalled strolling with Brzezinski near where the Berlin Wall once stood. The occasion was a conference held by the

German ministry of defense. Zbig, as Avineri remembered it, said that he did not feel any nostalgia for the divided Berlin, but also did not feel any enthusiasm over the unification of Berlin. This was a reaction to the German triumphalism then on the rise, Avineri thought. He had similar feelings. He summed it up in these words: "An American with Polish roots and a Jew with Polish roots felt the same in reunified Berlin. That," he remarked, "is understandable for a Pole and a Jew, but not necessarily for the average American."

## Notes

"Brzezinski was a private individual . . . ": *Power and Principle*, p. 84.

Criticism by Ross: Ross, Dennis, and David Makovsky, *Myths, Illusions, and Peace. Finding a New Direction for America in the Middle East*, p.6.

"'Impose' means . . . ": Brzeziński, Zbigniew, and Brent Scowcroft, *America and the World. Conversations on the Future of American Foreign Policy. Moderated by David Ignatius*, p. 80.

Isolating Hamas: ibid., p. 86.

"When I first went to the Middle East . . . ": ibid., p. 90.

"If I were an Israeli . . . ": ibid.

Brzezinski on Sadat: *Power and Principle*, p. 93.

Carter's willingness: ibid., p. 97.

"I was presented as anti-Israeli . . . ": ibid, p. 98.

"I was deeply touched . . . ": ibid., p. 100.

# PUBLIC ENEMY #1

"Most of my mature life was spent on strategizing how to undermine the Soviet bloc," said Brzezinski in his discussion with Brent Scowcroft and David Ignatius. The statement came as a surprise to no one in Moscow.

Brzezinski did not spend eternity digging in the archives like some or sweat over a book for twenty years like others. He did not fill his desk drawer with manuscripts. When he talked, it wasn't in a whisper or to himself. No convoluted rhetorical flourishes or arcane allegories. You knew what he liked and what he didn't like. Moscow took note of him early and kept an eye on him.

It's not hard to understand why Moscow didn't like Brzezinski. He kept holding a mirror up to the Kremlin's face. He analyzed totalitarianism with its inhuman mechanisms for abasing and trampling human dignity. He reminded the USSR of what it wanted to forget: the horrid years of Stalinism, purges, and deporting whole nations. Even worse, he compared the Soviet system to Hitler's totalitarian rule. "What happened under Stalin," he wrote in *Grand Failure*, "wasn't a distortion of the system, but its essence. Stalin did not betray Lenin. He faithfully continued his work."

Earlier, in his 1970 book *Between Two Ages: America's Role in the Technetronic Era*, Brzezinski stated that "despite the extraordinarily detailed and gory accounts of Stalin's crimes made available to the entire Soviet public during the Twenty-Second Congress of the

Communist Party of the Soviet Union in 1961, the tendency of the post-Khrushchev Soviet leaders has been to minimize Stalin's misdeeds and to stress the accomplishments of the thirties. The implication is that the party acted correctly throughout and hence that its claim to power is derived from the essentially infallible leadership it has provided both in the past and in the present."

He talked about "the bureaucratization of boredom."

> *The Communist Party of the Soviet Union has a unique achievement to its credit: it has succeeded in transforming the most important revolutionary doctrine of our age into dull social and political orthodoxy. That orthodoxy is revolutionary in rhetoric but conservative in practice. The political system, highly centralized but arrested in its development, is seen by some Soviet citizens as increasingly irrelevant to the needs of Soviet society, as frozen in an ideological posture that was a response to an altogether different age.... Indeed, the ultimate irony is that the Soviet political system—having thrust Russia into the mid-industrial age—has now become the principal impediment to the country's further evolution. It keeps Russia in a mold that is industrial bourgeois socially and dogmatic authoritarian politically. For the USSR to become a truly modern society, the basic assumptions and structure of the political forms created to press industrialization must be changed.*

Brzezinski snatched away communism's fig leaf. He wrote about Russia's autocratic traditions and the role of violence there before and after the revolution, questioning the idea that the revolution was a dramatic break with the past. With cold precision, he unmasked the two fundamental weaknesses of the USSR: immanent economic paralysis and the ethnic conflicts fermenting under the thin surface.

# ZBIG

In the summer of 1968, in *Neues Deutschland*, the East German party newspaper, Brzezinski was accused of seeking to influence developments in Czechoslovakia. The paper referred to his June 14, 1968, lecture in Prague where he supposedly advised his audience to erase the Leninism in Marxism-Leninism and said that "the facts prove that one must speak of political interference of imperialist forces in the internal affairs of Czechoslovakia."

Commenting on that attack in the *New York Times*, Brzezinski, then director of the Institute for the Study of Communism at Columbia University, said it was symptomatic that the East German regime was singling him out to attack rather than "those who oppose East-West reconciliation," and added that "only dogmatic Communists who desire continued Cold War and are willing to run the risk of nuclear confrontation would disagree with my views. It puts them in the same category as the extreme right wing in this country."

He was one of the first advocates of détente but did not want the Soviets to be given a menu to pick and choose from—détente where it was convenient and fierce competition where they saw American weakness or indecisiveness.

The Carter-Brzezinski team, inspired by the latter, abandoned the Nixon-Kissinger-Ford policies that relied on avoiding ideological disputes in mutual relations. From the outset of his term, Carter meddled in Soviet internal affairs. The Kremlin hated him for this. Even more so, it hated the architect of this fundamental change in American policy.

On January 20, 1977, the day of Jimmy Carter's inauguration, the US President received a letter from Andrei Sakharov, a Soviet nuclear physicist, dissident, and human rights activist. Sakharov wrote: "It's very important to defend those who suffer because of their nonviolent struggle for an open society, for justice, for other people whose rights are violated. It is our duty and yours to fight for them. I think that a lot depends on this struggle—trust between peoples, confidence in lofty promises, and, in the final analysis, international security."

Sakharov did more than report on the way dissidents were being persecuted, terrorized, and murdered. The letter concluded with a plea for the president to "take steps in this regard in the international arena."

Before he was even sworn in, the president-elect sent a telegram of support to Soviet dissident Vladimir Slepak, and on December 22, Cyrus Vance received Andrei Amalrik, who had been expelled from the USSR. Immediately after the inauguration, the State Department accused Czechoslovakia of human rights violations. The next day, it warned that attempts to intimidate Sakharov "stand in contradiction to accepted international human rights standards."

To the degree that Moscow could still cherish some illusions as to Washington's determination during the first year of the Carter administration, the following year saw a turn toward confrontation. The American press saw Brzezinski as the architect of the hard line. There was a belief that Cyrus Vance counseled patience while Brzezinski saw it as a mistake to tolerate Soviet interference in Africa. Carter was tacking increasingly close to the course Brzezinski set.

On June 7, 1978, in a commencement address at the US Naval Academy in Annapolis, President Jimmy Carter said: "The Soviet Union can choose either confrontation or cooperation. The United States is adequately prepared to meet either choice."

No one in the Kremlin had doubts as to the authorship of those words. Brzezinski swears that Carter wrote his own speech.

> *In fact, the speech was largely Carter's own handiwork. . . . . Contrary to subsequent press accounts, it was the President himself who labeled the Soviets as having a totalitarian and repressive regime, who inserted unfavorable comparisons between the United States and the Soviet Union, and who posed the stark*

*choice of "cooperation or confrontation." I thought that Vance would object to these insertions, and I therefore did not recommend that they be struck out, though my own inclination would have been to omit them and to insert instead stronger language on Soviet military activities by proxy in the Third World.*

On June 17, 1978 the communist party organ *Pravda* published an article accusing Washington of heating up the arms race, drawing closer to China against Soviet interests, intervening militarily in Africa, and stalling on disarmament talks. The conclusion: "The main source of this worsening of the situation is the increasing aggressiveness of Carter administration policies and the increasingly sharp anti-Soviet tone of statements by the president himself and his closest colleagues—above all Brzezinski." It later turned out that the article was based on a Politburo statement that Brezhnev had read out.

> *Columnist Max Lerner writes: "Brezhnev has chosen his target carefully. He knows that Brzezinski is feared as being too tough on the Russians by the tender-minded among the liberals in the media. He also knows that there is an anti-Brzezinski group in the State Department, in Congress, and even inside the National Security Council, which he heads. Long years of infighting within the Politburo have bred a skillful maneuverer in Brezhnev. The way to destroy Brzezinski's policies is to isolate him from the media, from Congress, from Carter himself."*
>
> *The evidence is not hard to find that Brezhnev's pinch of pepper is being reflected in sneezes throughout the pro-Soviet apparatus.*
>
> *The Daily World, successor to the Daily Worker, has a front-page editorial entitled: "Remove Brzezinski." The editorial quotes Gus Hall, general secretary of the Communist*

*party, USA, in a denunciation of Brzezinski, including the statement that Brzezinski is a "nuclear maniac."*

*What precipitated all of this? Little doubt can exist that it was Brzezinski's trip to the People's Republic of China.... Already the Soviets have committed a considerable share of their military strength to a border watch adjoining China. While this continues, the Russian military presence available to confront NATO forces in western Europe is reduced.*

*Thus, all that the Soviet government can do to cause Brzezinski to lose his job or his influence it is doing....*

*Interestingly, Mr. Brzezinski has managed to turn the tables. Normally, the Soviets act and we react. Now it is we who have taken the initiative, and Mr. Brezhnev and his followers are forced into the role of responding to an accomplished fact of our devising.*

*Summary: Brzezinski's strategy has succeeded to the extent that he is now personally targeted by the Soviets. Those who take part in the vendetta against him will be serving the Soviet goals, even if unwittingly.*

On July 11, 1978, the Soviet ambassador to Washington, Anatoly Dobrynin sent the Soviet Foreign Minister Andrei Gromyko a letter reviewing the basic elements of Soviet-American relations. Dobrynin informed his boss about Carter's decision to "carry out a regular reevaluation of Soviet-American relations." The initiative—writes Dobrynin—came from Brzezinski and several presidential advisers on domestic affairs, who convinced Carter that he would arrest the deterioration of his stand in the country if he would openly initiate a harsher course vis-à-vis the Soviet Union.

However, writes Dobrynin, "Carter became convinced that détente is not a 'faucet' which he can turn on and off whenever he feels so disposed" and that "the President, having let Vance go out front, decided to restrain Brzezinski a bit."

Dobrynin reports that "the Carter Administration has come to its own variety of a selective, half-hearted conception of détente (of which Brzezinski himself first accused us)."

"Special attention has lately been assigned," writes Dobrynin, "to the Administration's policy towards China, which according to all signs bears witness—if not formally, then in essence—to its yearning for a plot with China against the interests of the Soviet Union. The danger of this course to our interests is self-evident. Brzezinski, whom Gus Hall named 'the Carter regime's Rasputin,' continues to play a significant role in all of this."

Dobrynin knew that the dig would go down well with his Kremlin colleagues. No American was so insufferable to them as Brzezinski.

The late spring and summer of 1978 were a time of tension on various fronts. Moscow's relations with China were rapidly deteriorating while the USSR-Vietnam alliance was tightening. On August 12, Japan and China signed a treaty of peace and friendship.

The KGB had its hands full. Jewish dissident Vladimir Slepak was sentenced to five years of internal exile and, soon after, Aleksandr Ginzburg to eight years of hard labor for anti-Soviet propaganda. Anatoly Sharansky got "only" thirteen years for "treason, espionage, and anti-Soviet activity." Anatoly Filatov was sentenced to death for espionage.

Differences of opinion emerged in the Carter administration over how to respond to this wave of repression. Brzezinski favored limiting trade and, especially, technology transfers. Defense Secretary Harold Brown and the president's domestic political advisers backed him. Secretary of State Vance and Treasury Secretary Michael Blumenthal led the opposition. The Brzezinski group won. America also put two Moscow spies employed by the UN, who did not have diplomatic immunity, on trial. They were both sentenced to 50 years in prison. Both the State Department and the CIA had opposed the arrests and trials.

Relations began gradually improving in the fall. Hopes of a miraculous thaw evaporated and a sense of realism returned. US–Soviet trade set a new record of $2.8 billion in 1978. Yet Moscow's trade with West Germany was exactly twice as large, at $5.6 billion.

West German Chancellor Helmut Schmidt was no fan of Brzezinski's, and Brzezinski returned the sentiment. On one occasion, Schmidt greeted him with "Hi, Zbig," and Brzezinski shot back, "Hi, Helmut," which displeased the chancellor for reasons that are not entirely clear.

During Schmidt's July 1977 visit to Washington, at a State Department luncheon, the chancellor made the argument that the United States should be more responsive to the "good Brezhnev who is promoting détente and who needs our help."

Carter was not enthusiastic about the idea. Schmidt may very well have blamed the "Polish hawk" for this, and afterward things went downhill. In 1979, relations deteriorated sharply over the deployment of medium-range nuclear missiles in Western Europe as a response to the Soviet SS-20. The German chancellor surprised the Americans by questioning prior NATO agreements. His stance may have resulted from lobbying by German industry, which traditionally counseled against irritating the Kremlin, especially with trade flourishing. Shortly thereafter, Schmidt accepted Brezhnev's invitation to discuss issues including Afghanistan, despite the fact that Washington viewed the visit inappropriate. On his return, Schmidt used a conversation with individuals close to Carter to urge the president to get rid of Brzezinski on the grounds that he was an obstacle to East-West relations. The president informed Zbig of the conversation.

In his 1995 book *In Confidence*, Dobrynin indirectly admitted that Brzezinski was right by characterizing the decision to deploy SS-20 rockets in the western USSR as "stupid." Dobrynin felt that the 1979 American response, putting Pershing and cruise missiles in Europe, tipped the nuclear balance in favor of the United States.

Although Dobrynin had no intention of praising Brzezinski, he did admit that the "soft" Western response to the 1968 invasion of Czechoslovakia encouraged Moscow to attack Afghanistan. He might well have added that the fact they paid no price in Angola in 1975, in the days of Ford and Kissinger, was an inducement for Soviet involvement in the Arabian Peninsula several years later. Brzezinski was determined to prevent that conflict from being a rerun of Angola. Gromyko proposed joint Soviet-American mediation in 1978. Brzezinski said no for two reasons. In the first place, it smelled like a condominium, and in the second, it would have legitimized a Soviet presence in the region. The rivalry over Yemen was full of intrigue and lethal covert action. Before the Americans knew it, the Cubans were training the army, the East Germans instructing the security forces, and North Yemen was playing host to 200 Soviet military advisers, 60 jet fighters, and several hundred Soviet and Polish tanks.

In 1980, Romuald Spasowski, the Polish ambassador in Washington, told Brzezinski that American communists had asked for his help in collecting information to use against Brzezinski. They had supposedly also eavesdropped on Brzezinski's conversations with the pope—but not for their own sake, nor on their own initiative.

When Carter named Senator Edmund Muskie to replace Vance after the fiasco of the operation to rescue the Tehran hostages, *Time* wrote on May 12, 1980 that

> he [Vance] would have liked to serve out his term, partly because he has never thought of himself as a quitter but also because he wanted to play a key part in what he sees as the biggest challenge facing the Carter Administration in foreign policy: salvaging détente.... Perhaps Carter's conviction that right makes might—that morality, truth, and trust matter so much in politics—prevented him from viewing the Soviet

*Union more pragmatically at the outset, then caused him to overreact when the Soviets invaded Afghanistan. Carter's lack of an intuitive grasp of how to deal with the Soviets, combined with his righteous wrath over their misbehavior, has made him all the more susceptible to what Vance sees as Brzezinski's excessive reliance on punitive policies. Vance has supported the post-Afghanistan sanctions, but he believes that the US must start talking to the Soviets again about how to rebuild détente and save SALT. However, he recognizes that perhaps first there had to be a clearing of the air, an end to nonstop stories about his feud with Brzezinski, and a resolution—in favor of the Secretary of State —of who is the President's principal foreign policy adviser. Vance is confident that Ed Muskie will assert himself with, and over, Brzezinski, and that Muskie shares Vance's approach to US-Soviet relations.*

*Time* quoted analysts, saying, "Moscow was greatly relieved that the job would not go to Brzezinski, a man who they feel is a Soviet-hater by nature and who is often attacked in the Soviet press as a peddler of 'slander and obvious lies.' "

The feeling of relief, however, was premature. Ronald Reagan respected Brzezinski and listened to what he had to say. He considered entrusting him with the same post—adviser to the president for National Security. His campaign chairman and later CIA chief, William Casey, was said to be "for," but Casper Weinberger and George Schultz were against.

Zbig's book *Game Plan* swept Washington off its feet when it came out in 1986, and Reagan phoned Brzezinski with congratulations. Casper Weinberger sent a commendatory letter from the Pentagon. National Security Adviser Admiral John Poindexter made it required reading for his staff.

In the summer of 1989, when the Soviet Union was already staggering, Foreign Minister Eduard Shevardnadze complained to

James Baker, secretary of state in the George H. W. Bush administration, that "I know that there are some in your society, like Brzezinski, who would like to exploit Soviet troubles. His forecast of the end of socialism and the need to take advantage of this is shared by others.... We won't allow destabilization in the Soviet Union—destabilization in such a huge country with enormous military and economic potential would have been a grave thing for the Soviet Union and the world."

The list of Brzezinski's political opponents was long and highly varied.

Noam Chomsky, a cult figure for the radical left, attributed far more power to Brzezinski than Zbig possessed (although not as much, wags said, as he dreamed of having).

In *La verdadera historia del club Bilderberg* (The True Story of the Bilderberg Group), a book by Daniel Estulin, Spain-based journalist, Brzezinski's name, as a key operator of the world conspiracy, appears more frequently than any other except Kissinger's and David Rockefeller's. A reader learns that Wall Street stood behind Lenin and the Bolshevik revolution. "Had the Bolshevik Revolution failed, Russia's industrial development would surely have rivaled that of the United States, Great Britain, and Europe, and we would have been living in a very different world today. But, by supporting the Bolshevik Revolution, American financiers slowed down Russian industrial growth to a snail's pace in the lead-up to World War II."

The book has been translated into 24 languages, and was in its 15th printing when I read it.

On March 14, 2007, the Economist Blog referred to "a new brain for Barack Obama": "It's 78 years old and it still works perfectly. It belongs to Zbigniew Brzezinski, the peppery ex-national security adviser to Jimmy Carter."

Others were less generous, although they saw Brzezinski as the real power behind the throne to be.

In February, 2008, the website of Jeff Rense, an American conspiracy theorist and radio talk-show host, reported that "the Illinois Senator is a synthetic Manchurian candidate who has been concocted over a period of two decades or more by a political intelligence faction associated with the Zbigniew Brzezinski clan, and Zbig's friends of the 'color revolutions' faction at the National Endowment for Democracy and the Soros milieu."

In the summer of 2008, Eric Walberg, a self-proclaimed expert on "postmodern imperialism" and a contributor to *Al-Ahram Weekly*, argued on the same website.

> *It is hard to sort through the hype and heat of Obamamania, but one thing is clear: who's pulling the strings. It is—you got it—Brzezinski. . . .*
>
> *What's especially ghoulish about all this is that there are five Brzezinski offspring who are all on board the Obama wagon: Mark (director of Russian and Eurasian Affairs at the National Security Council under President Bill Clinton, and one of the prime movers of the 2004 color revolution in Ukraine), Ian (currently the US Deputy Assistant Secretary of State for European and NATO affairs and a backer of Kosovan independence, NATO expansion into Ukraine and Georgia and US ABM missiles in Poland), Mika (political commentator on MSNBC whose interview with Michele Obama contributed to the general media Obamamania) and finally, Matthew (a friend of Ilyas Akhmadov, "foreign minister" and US envoy of the Chechen opposition). . . .*

Walburg concludes: "Obama is literally a second chance for Brzezinski: having destroyed the Soviet Union and shattered the Warsaw Pact, he now wants to dismember the Russian Federation itself and put the finishing touches on Afghanistan as an impregnable US military base against China, Russia . . . the list is endless.

Perhaps Zbig is dreaming of restoring Greater Poland circa 1600—from the Black Sea to the Baltic, all controlled by petty *szlachta* aristocrats like . . . the Brzezinskis?"

## Notes

The bureaucratization of boredom: Zbigniew K. Brzezinski, *Between Two Ages: America's Role in the Technetronic Era* (Westport, CT: Praeger Publishers, 1982), 57.

Carter's authorship of the "cooperation or confrontation" speech: Zbigniew Brzezinski, *Power and Principle: Memoirs of the National Security Adviser, 1977–1981* (New York: Farrar, Strauss and Giroux, 1983), 320–321.

Lerner: *The Spokesman Review*, July 5, 1978.

Schmidt's luncheon praise of Brezhnev: *Power and Principle*, 307.

Shevardnadze to Baker: James A. Baker III with Thomas M. DeFrank, *The Politics of Diplomacy: Revolution, War, and Peace, 1989–1992* (New York: G.P. Putnam's Sons, 1995), 139.

# POLAND:
# 1980 AND AFTERWARD

---

December 2010. Al Jazeera broadcasts One on One with Zbigniew Brzezinski—an interview almost half an hour long, richly illustrated with photos from the Brzezinski family album. The interviewer keeps going back to Zbig's Polish roots. The interviewee repeatedly reminds him that he spent only three years in his home country, from the age of seven to ten, and that, although he remembered military parades, little remained when he visited Warsaw for the first time after the war in 1957 except for certain smells and the awareness that he came from there. At the same time, the war, the loss of Polish independence, and the enormous violence inflicted on his native country all influenced the way he saw the world and made him sensitive to the fact that conflicts make up a large part of international politics, and conflicts must be managed wisely. As a student and teacher at Harvard, he recalls, he came to understand that America should aim for victory in the Cold War while refraining from military force, an uncertain method with unforeseeable consequences.

When he found himself in the White House, he militated from the beginning against treating all the Eastern European countries the same. He never believed that the Soviet bloc was a monolith.

He also urged a serious approach to the Helsinki Final Act, which Moscow signed at the Conference on Security and Cooperation in Europe, demanding that it be respected.

In his first report for President Carter on February 19, 1977, Brzezinski noted that on February 15 the Board for International Broadcasting and the Portuguese government had signed a fifteen-year extension for the basing of Radio Free Europe transmitters, which would also be able to broadcast Radio Liberty. "For the United States, these radio stations are the most important means of access to the countries of the USSR and Eastern Europe."

Madeleine Albright recalls that when Edmund Muskie—a politician with Polish origins, former governor, presidential candidate, and chairman of the Senate Budget Committee—replaced Cyrus Vance as secretary of state, he felt that Brzezinski treated him superciliously.

> *After one contentious meeting—writes Albright—Muskie asked, "Why does your boss feel the need to show off in front of the president? Who cares if he knows the name of every tribe in Nigeria?" "He's not showing off," I replied. "He's a professor, and professors are trained to know facts."*
>
> *For his part, Brzezinski complained, "Why doesn't your friend Muskie do anything at meetings except ask questions? We need to know what he thinks." I explained, "He's a senator. Senators ask questions. They don't take positions until they have to, and they don't have to until there's a vote." The two even quarreled who was more Polish—a fight Brzezinski won because he was born in Poland and knew the language. Muskie had a Polish father but was born in Maine—not the same thing.*

Adam Michnik, the Polish opposition leader who first met Brzezinski as an eighteen-year-old in Munich in 1964, said that the encounter with the Kennedy aide and author of *Unity and Conflict* was a formative experience. "To this day, I cannot comprehend why he took me seriously," he says. More than a dozen years later, when Michnik was serving time in a communist prison, a Spanish newspaper published an article about how Brzezinski was trying to tear the satellite countries free of the Soviet embrace, and that Michnik was acting on his orders. This was the last thing Michnik needed. He sent Brzezinski a letter from prison saying, "I urge you, sir, to correct this information." Zbig called a press conference where he declared "this shows how the Warsaw authorities harass opposition activists and the methods they will sink to. It is a clear KGB provocation."

"In Warsaw, they flew into a rage," Michnik remembers. "The warden called me in and said, 'Listen, Michnik, you sent that letter to Brzezinski.' " The prisoner replied, "I don't know anything about it." The warden said, "Radio Free Europe reported it," and the prisoner shot back, "I don't listen to Radio Free Europe in prison. And I'm surprised that you do."

"Later I had several chances to meet Zbig and make friends with him," Michnik says. "More than what he said, because we didn't agree on everything—for instance, he was far more skeptical about perestroika than me—I was fascinated by his capacity for synthesis, his realism, his fervent heart and his cool head. Talking to Zbig is an unending lesson in political thinking. No empty phrases or banalities. No slogans, romantic gestures, or complaining about injustices."

Brzezinski observed the strikes in Poland, the rise of Solidarity, and everything that followed with a mixture of joy, excitement, and misgivings. On the one hand, his prediction that the system would begin to crumble from within was coming true. Among Solidarity's advisers were people he knew, respected, and tried to help. On the other hand, he knew like few others what would happen in the Kremlin.

On August 25, 1980, at Brzezinski's suggestion, Carter sent a letter to Margaret Thatcher, Valéry Giscard d'Estaing, and Helmut Kohl indicating the possibility of Soviet intervention in Poland.

On September 3, Brzezinski commissioned a report on a possible invasion from Admiral Stansfield Turner, the head of the CIA. On September 19, Turner submitted an "alert" memo on Soviet military movements.

In Moscow on December 1, Marshal Nikolai Ogarkov, chief of the Soviet general staff, showed representatives of the Polish general staff the details of Warsaw Pact maneuvers and informed them that eighteen divisions—fifteen, Soviet; two, Czechoslovakian; and one, East German—were prepared to cross the Polish borders on December 8.

On December 3, Brzezinski drafted a private warning from Carter to Brezhnev, which was sent on the hot line from the White House to the Kremlin the same day. It stated that the United States wished neither to take advantage of events in Poland nor to threaten Soviet security in Eastern Europe, but that the imposition of a solution on the Polish people by force would lead to a marked worsening of mutual relations. Carter sent another message via the hot line on December 7. It contained a warning that any intervention in Poland could result in the transfer of advanced American weapons to China.

The main thing for Carter and Brzezinski was to make the old men in the Kremlin understand that although an invasion would not lead to the launching of American rockets, there would nevertheless be a stiff price to pay for such an escapade, and so they should think twice, or even three times, before issuing the order.

On December 8, Brzezinski wrote in his journal:

> *I see four objectives to what we are doing: one is to deprive the Soviets of surprise. This we have already done. Two, perhaps to encourage the Poles to resist, if they are not taken by*

*surprise, for this might somehow deter the Soviets. The publicity is already doing that. Thirdly and paradoxically, to calm the situation in Poland by making the Poles more aware that the Soviets may in fact enter. The Poles have till now discounted this possibility and this may have emboldened them excessively. Here in effect we have a common interest with the Soviets, for they too may prefer to intimidate the Poles to a degree. And fourth, to deter the Soviet from coming in, by intensifying international pressure and condemnation of the Soviet Union.*

Brzezinski wrote in his memoirs that he "conferred with Lane Kirkland of the AFL-CIO, and we agreed that a worldwide boycott to the shipment of the Soviet Union of any goods, by air, rail, or sea, should be organized—Kirkland seemed reasonably optimistic that there would be widespread international support—and I sent a memorandum to the Department of Defense instructing it to prepare lists of weapons that might be transferred by the United States to China in the event of a Soviet invasion of Poland. Knowing the Defense Department, I felt fairly confident that the substance of this memorandum would rapidly become more publicly known."

With the President's approval he phoned the Pope and briefed him on the situation. In his memoirs, Brzezinski wrote that "in a way the conversation was historically unique. Here was the Assistant for National Security Affairs to the President of the United States conferring with the Roman Pontiff in the Vatican in Polish about peace and Poland."

In Report No. 160 to the president, Brzezinski wrote that

*We have a seemingly reliable account of what transpired in Moscow, based on a debrief by the Polish Foreign Minister who attended. In essence, Kania (head of the Polish Communist Party) was generally confident in early December that his handling of the Polish problem had sufficiently reassured the Soviets that a repetition of Czechoslovakia was not likely. He was thus taken aback when the sudden invitation to Moscow was issued. At the Summit, the sole item was whether "Poland needed external 'help' in the form of military intervention." Kania argued strongly against it, arguing that the Party could resolve the issue and that in the event that it could not he would be prepared to seek Soviet help. In the discussions, the Czechs and the East Germans argued for providing "help," while Hungary and Romania argued against it. In the argument the latter two were eventually joined by Bulgaria. Brezhnev made it clear that the Soviet Union was willing to "help" provided the Warsaw Pact was in favor of it.*

Brzezinski noted in his diary for December 15, 1980, a dispatch from Brussels stating that West Germany opposed efforts by other states (Britain, France, and the United States) to agree economic sanctions against the Soviet Union in case of intervention. The Germans consented only to plans for a crisis situation. France stated unequivocally that French public opinion would demand a strong reaction whether the government wanted one or not. They also demanded the suspension of arms control talks by Washington. Brzezinski noted that this confirmed his suspicions about the ongoing Finlandization of Germany.

General Wojciech Jaruzelski declared martial law—a "state of war"—in Poland a year later. We will never know for sure whether this scenario was inevitable, or the degree to which Brzezinski's efforts protected the Poles from an earlier, bloodier outcome.

On November 20, 1980, shortly after Carter lost the election, CIA head Turner presented an intelligence report to president-elect Reagan. It assessed the situation in Poland. Bob Woodward writes in his 1987 book *The Veil* that

> *Turner was tempted to disclose, but he did not, that the CIA had a deep-penetration spy, a colonel on the Polish General Staff, who provided a steady flow of intelligence out of Warsaw on the intentions of the Poles and the Soviets. The colonel's sensitive reports were circulated on a BIGOT list only to the most senior US officials who had an absolute need to know. [The codename "BIGOT," derived from the words "To Gib" dates back to World War II when Allied orders for officers were stamped TO GIB for those being sent to Gibraltar for preparations for the invasion of North Africa; later their orders were stamped BIG OT—TO GIB backward—when they were sent back to begin planning Operation Overlord, the invasion of Normandy.] Carter, Vice-President Walter F. Mondale, and Brzezinski were the only ones from the White House with the regular BIGOT-list access. The colonel's name, Kuklinski, was never included in these reports, and only few CIA officers knew it.*

When Brzezinski met Ryszard Kuklinski in the Four Seasons Hotel, he told him, "You have served Poland well." Later, Brzezinski joined the Polish ambassador to the United States at the time, Jerzy Kozminski, in long months of efforts to have Kuklinski rehabilitated.

At a conference outside Warsaw in November 1997, former Warsaw Pact Supreme Commander Marshal Viktor Kulikov spoke dismissively of the significance of the information that Kuklinski provided. Brzezinski retorted that in the event of a Soviet attack on NATO, thanks to that information, the entire Soviet staff, including Kulikov, would have been dead within three hours. Kulikov looked impressed.

In the fall of 1989, Brzezinski visited Moscow at the invitation of the Soviet Academy of Sciences. He addressed a packed auditorium on "the common European home" and the fact that it would not be common as long as parts of it remained behind a wall. The audience responded with a standing ovation. On this trip, Brzezinski asked Aleksandr Yakovlev, the chief ideologue of perestroika and glasnost, for permission to visit Katyn. On November 1, he arrived there in the company of American ambassador Jack F. Matlock Jr. and *Time* correspondent Strobe Talbott. Brzezinski recalls that a local party dignitary handed him a wreath with a ribbon reading "To the Polish Officers, Victims of German Criminals, 1941." Brzezinski tore off the ribbon in anger and wrote in large letters on a sheet of paper, "To the Polish Officers, Victims of Stalin and the NKVD." His host stood stiffly and turned pale.

Soviet television filmed the wreath and asked Brzezinski for his comments. Alluding to the presence at the ceremony of members of the Katyn Victims Family association, he said that "it was not my personal pain that brought me here, as in the case of most of those present, but rather an awareness of the historical nature of Katyn. Russians and Poles rest here together. For me, it is important to tell the truth about what happened here, because only together with the truth can the new Soviet leadership distance itself from the crimes of Stalin and the NKVD. Only truth can serve as a basis for genuine friendship between the nations of the USSR and Poland. Truth will always find a way. I am strengthened in this belief by the very fact that I could come here."

The local dignitary sighed with relief and even smiled.

When communism ended in Poland in 1989, voices were heard opining that it might be a good idea for Brzezinski to run for the presidency of the independent nation. I asked Adam Michnik, the head of the country's largest paper today, about this. Michnik recalled the words of the late Jan Nowak-Jezioranski, former head of the Polish section of Radio Free Europe and a friend of Zbig's, who said that Brzezinski would never run, in part because it might make the country of his birth look ridiculous—couldn't a worthy candidate be found among its almost 40 million residents? Beyond that, running for president would only provide ammunition for those who had unreasonably stated down the years that everything Brzezinski did resulted from his Polish origins.

## Notes

Madeleine Albright, *Memo to the President Elect: How We Can Restore, America's Reputation and Leadership* (New York: HarperCollins, 2008).

On the phone call to the Vatican: Zbigniew Brzezinski, *Power and Principle: Memoirs of the National Security Adviser, 1977–1981* (New York: Farrar, Straus and Giroux, 1983), 466–467.

On Brzezinski's defense of Kuklinski and Kulikov's reaction: Benjamin Weiser, *A Secret Life: The Polish Officer, His Covert Mission, and the Price He Paid to Save His Country* (New York: PublicAffairs, 2004).

# ONCE AGAIN, NO ILLUSIONS

**"Drinking Coca-Cola does not make Russians think any more like Americans than eating sushi makes Americans think like Japanese," Samuel Huntington, Brzezinski's colleague at Harvard, and later his subordinate on the National Security Council, noted some time ago.**

Likewise, the freedom to travel, to worship, to speak out, and to use the Internet doesn't make Russia a democracy. The presence of a stock exchange does not make it a market economy, either.

*History can be reduced to farce, especially if it serves a political purpose. After the unexpectedly abrupt end of the Cold War, millions of American were repeatedly told that the defeat of Soviet communism was the doing of just one man. In its simplest rendering, this version of history could resemble a fairy tale, perhaps like this one: Once upon a time on Planet Earth there was an Evil Empire seeking global domination. But when confronted by Ronald, the prince from the Republic of Freedom, the empire recoiled and before long, on December 26, 1991, its blood-stained red flag was lowered from the towering ramparts of the Kremlin castle. The Evil Empire had abjectly surrendered, and the Republic of Freedom lived happily ever after.*

"Almost in a deterministic Marxist fashion, the growth of democracy in Russia was expected to be largely a product of market forces rather than an outgrowth of deeper philosophical or spiritual values."

> Bush underestimated the genuine depth of non-Russian nationalism within the faltering state and was seduced by the notion that the Soviet Union was synonymous with Russia. . . . The administration's misconceptions on this score were reflected in President Bush's infamous "Chicken Kiev" speech (given that merciless name by New York Times columnist William Safire), delivered in August 1991 in Ukraine's capital, with thousands of Ukrainians hoping to hear the president of the world's leading democracy endorse their aspirations to independence. To their bafflement, they heard instead that "freedom is not the same as independence. Americans will not support those who seek independence in order to replace a far-off tyranny with local despotism. They will not aid those who promote a suicidal nationalism bases upon ethnic hatred."

In those days, Washington's policy toward Russia, Brzezinski says, was rich in rhetoric, magnanimous in gestures, but empty from the point of view of strategy. "Boris Yeltsin was hailed as a great democratic leader; partly to compensate for the cold shoulder Bush gave him during his rise to power so as not to offend Gorbachev. But not much thought was given to developing a comprehensive program for political and socioeconomic transformation that would firmly link Russia to Europe."

Swiftly flowing stream of American money was indeed gushing into Russia, but the majority of it was simply stolen.

On October 10, 1997, before the Senate Foreign Relations Committee, Brzezinski voiced strong support for NATO enlargement.

# ZBIG

*In brief, to me NATO expansion is not principally about the Russian threat, for currently it does not exist, though one cannot exclude its reappearance and hence some insurance against it is desirable. Secondly, to me NATO expansion is not primarily a moral crusade, meant to undo the injustice the Central European peoples suffered during the half-century-long Soviet oppression, though one cannot ignore the moral right of the newly emancipated and democratic Central Europeans to a life no less secure than that enjoyed by the West Europeans. For me, the central stake in NATO expansion is the long-term historic and strategic relationship between America and Europe. NATO expansion is central to the vitality of the American-European connection, to the scope of a democratic and secure Europe, and to the ability of America and Europe to work together in promoting international security.*

Brzezinski was a vocal and effective advocate of this idea, which had many opponents in America. He neither turned a blind eye to Russian behavior nor stopped speaking out about it in a ringing voice.

On October 6, 1999, he testified again to the Senate Foreign Relations Committee. This time, his testimony was on the lessons of Kosovo. The bottom line: the current Russian government is not trustworthy.

He presented evidence, even if he labeled it circumstantial, of collusion between Russia and Serbia. Even prior to the NATO bombing, the Duma, Russia's parliament, called for aid to Yugoslavia if NATO struck. When the air attack began, Russia sought UN condemnation, and Prime Minister Primakov attempted to split off the Germans with a peace proposal that was much more favorable to Slobodan Milosevic than NATO's. (Two years earlier, in charge of Russian foreign affairs—he had previously been the intelligence chief—he followed up the introductory courtesies in a meeting with Madeleine Albright by telling her that thanks to his professional experience he knew everything about her and wanted to hear from her own lips whether, like her former mentor Professor Brzezinski, she was anti-Russian.)

In his testimony, Brzezinski talked about persistent rumors that a "volunteer" Russian contingent had gone to fight on the Serb side and quoted Western intelligence source reports on Russian military equipment deliveries to the Serbs. He recalled an article in a leading Moscow newspaper, *Nezavisimaya Gazeta*, from March 25, 1999. The paper triumphantly declared that the Kosovo action was initiating "the collapse of the US global empire" and that it was in Russia's interest to let "the United States and NATO with its demented West and East European members bog down as deep as possible in a Balkan war."

When it dawned on the Kremlin, said Brzezinski, that the NATO alliance would neither split nor quit, Russia shifted its stand and sought to be part of Western decision-making process. Former Prime Minister Viktor Chernomyrdin, as his country's special envoy, sought to convince NATO that it should soften its stand. However, he met with Milosevic alone, while Russia's public message became increasingly strident.

On May 27, 1999, Chernomyrdin, in an op-ed piece in the *Washington Post*, asserted that "the United States lost its moral right to be regarded as the leaders of the democratic world when its bombs shattered the ideals of liberty and democracy in Yugoslavia." He called for the payment of reparations to Belgrade, and warned that he would urge President Yeltsin to freeze all American-Russian relations unless the bombing stopped. The next day, he met alone with Milosevic.

When Milosevic accepted NATO's demand for the withdrawal of all Serb forces, Chernomyrdin in an interview with Russian TV stated that "at Yugoslavia's special request, Russia will also be represented" in the occupying peacekeeping force.

The Russian foreign and defense ministers held a closed meeting with the Duma to reassure it that Yugoslavia had not been betrayed. The next day, Russian officers did not show up at the first scheduled encounter between NATO and Serbian officers, held to coordinate the Serb withdrawal. Soon after, a Russian military contingent moved toward Kosovo. As this was happening, the Russian government reassured Vice President Gore that the Russian troops would not enter Kosovo. A day later, at night, the Russian forces entered Pristina, Kosovo's capital, and took defensive positions at the airport, barring the later arriving NATO forces.

"A detailed account in the *Moskovskiy Komsomolets* tells the rest of the story," Brzezinski told the Senate Committee.

> *Crowing over the Russian military coup and over Serbian crowds in Pristina burning US and British flags, the paper said that a contingent of 2,500 Russian paratroopers was ready to be flown into Pristina, and that "it has already been decided that Russia will have its own sector" in Kosovo. The report noted that although Hungary had denied Russia its air space, "this is not a problem—Bulgaria, for example, gave the go-ahead. Our planes could make a detour—from the Russian coast over the Black Sea and Bulgaria straight to Kosovo." In other words, Kosovo would be partitioned by a unilateral fiat, whether NATO liked it or not.*

Things did not turn out so. Not only Hungary, a NATO member, but also Bulgaria and Romania refused access to their air space, and the Kremlin prudently decided not to risk having its air transports forced down. Finally, Russia reluctantly agreed to have its troops dispersed within the US, French, and German zones.

Brzezinski drew a straightforward conclusion:

> *Russia today is in the midst of political, economic, and social crisis. The Russian people want security, stability, and eventually prosperity. They do not share their political elite's preoccupation*

*with international prestige and they do not support its military adventurism, be it now in Chechnya or earlier in Afghanistan. Unfortunately, the present Russian leadership—every member of which would feel quite at home in a Soviet government if the Soviet Union still existed—is driven by nostalgia for global power status and by resentment against America's special international standing. That motivation not only explains the Russian conduct in Kosovo but it provides a key lesson that should be drawn from that particular experience: namely, that Russia is not yet a reliable partner.*

Then came Putin, and like a buzzard, or rather a hawk, Brzezinski followed Putin's every move.

He took a skeptical view of the perspective for the rapid democratization of Russia. The main reason for his skepticism was Putin. What do we know about him? "He's said the end of the Soviet Union was the greatest calamity of the twentieth century. Now that's a century in which there were two world wars in which hundreds of millions of people were killed; a century in which there was Hitlerism and the Holocaust; a century in which there was Stalinism and the gulag. But to him, the relatively peaceful dismantling of the Soviet Union was the greatest geopolitical calamity of the century."

During a discussion with Brent Scowcroft and David Ignatius in 2008, Brzezinski recalled an interview that Putin gave at the inception of his presidency, in which he spoke about his forebears.

*The person he admired the most in his own family was his grandfather. Who was his grandfather? That hasn't been picked up very much by the Western press. His grandfather was a security guard for Lenin and later for Stalin, in fact his food taster. This is the man Putin admires the most. Then, about a year after he became president, he went to an annual celebration where all the senior generals of the KGB*

> were assembled, retired and new ones. He walked in, stood in front of them, saluted, and said, "Comrades, mission number one accomplished." Maybe it was a joke. But remember, he came from the KGB elite, the KGB agents who were stationed abroad. These were the pampered children of the Soviet Union. They had access to Western books, they could travel abroad, they were trusted. They were on special missions. I can well imagine their mood as they watched the Soviet Union disintegrate. And I can well imagine that a group of them—vigorous, younger, ambitious—said, "That has to be brought under control." So my sense of Putin is that he is reacting to what happened. I don't think he has assimilated the fact that the old imperial system cannot be recreated. He's motivated a great deal by nostalgia.

Russia's attack on Georgia in August 2008 reminded Brzezinski of the Soviet aggression against Finland.

> Fundamentally at stake is what kind of role Russia will play in the new international system. Unfortunately, Putin is putting Russia on a course that is ominously similar to Stalin's and Hitler's in the late 1930s. Swedish foreign minister Carl Bildt has correctly drawn an analogy between Putin's "justification" for dismembering Georgia—because of the Russians in South Ossetia—to Hitler's tactics vis-à-vis Czechoslovakia to "free" the Sudeten Deutsch. Even more ominous is the analogy of what Putin is doing vis-à-vis Georgia to what Stalin did vis-à-vis Finland: subverting by use of force the sovereignty of a small democratic neighbor. In effect, morally and strategically, Georgia is the Finland of our day.

He warned that Moscow's aggression against Georgia cannot be read as an isolated incident. Putin and his comrades in the Kremlin do not accept post-Soviet reality. The stakes are high. Putin is riding a nationalistic wave.

> *The question the international community now confronts is how to respond to a Russia that engages in the blatant use of force with larger imperial designs in mind: to reintegrate the former Soviet space under the Kremlin's control and to cut Western access to the Caspian Sea and Central Asia by gaining control over the Baku/ Ceyhan pipeline that runs through Georgia. In brief, the stakes are very significant. At stake is access to oil as that resource grows ever more scarce and expensive and how a major power conducts itself in our newly inter-dependent world, conduct that should be based on accommodation and consensus, not on brute force.*

When asked in an interview with the *Huffington Post* in August 2008, after the invasion of Georgia, whether the West had an obligation to protect Georgia militarily, Brzezinski responded:

> *The question is not what obligation the West may have at the moment. The question is about our longer-term interest. If Russia, which misjudges its power and its capacities, embarks now on a blatantly nationalistic and imperialistic course, we will all suffer. Therefore it is all the more important that Russia be stopped now by mobilizing a concerted, global effort to oppose and condemn the Russian invasion. Ultimately, that could lead to economic and financial sanctions, though one would hope that other Russian leaders, including its business elite, will have cooler heads and be more aware of Russia's own vulnerabilities. Russia is not ready to sustain a new cold war.*

He noted on the same occasion that "this invasion of Georgia by Russia is a very sad commentary on eight years of self-delusion in the White House regarding Putin and his regime. Two memorable comments stand out. First, when Bush first met Putin and said he looked into his soul and could trust him. Second, not long ago, Condi Rice claimed that American relations with Russia have never been better in history!"

When the interviewer asked why Brzezinski had not mentioned Dmitry Medvedev even once, but instead only Putin, and whether Medvedev had any role in all this, Zbig replied: "As much to do with it as the formal head of state of the Soviet Union in 1950 had to do with the running of the Soviet government. Does anyone remember his name? But the real ruler of the Soviet Union had a name that most still remember—and it rhymes with Putin."

For the Russian elite, acknowledging the independence of Abkhazia and South Ossetia was revenge for Kosovo—and that elite regarded what had happened in Kosovo as the nadir of Russian humiliation. The dispute over gas with Ukraine in January 2009, which cut Western European clients off from the shipments they had ordered, was intended to convince the West that Ukraine was unreliable.

Putin's dallying, before the price of oil skyrocketed, resulted from a simple calculation.

> *Given the rise of China to the east (with China's economy already five times larger than Russia's and its population nine times larger), the mounting hostility of the 300-or so million Muslims to the south (likely to increase to well over 400 million over the next two decades), and Russia's own economic weakness and demographic crisis (with Russian population already down to 145 million and dropping further) Russia literally had no choice. Rivalry with America was senseless, and an alliance with China would have meant subordination. . . . To be sure, in the near future—for a decade or so—it is altogether unlikely that Russia could become a member of NATO.*

*Not only will it take time for Russia to meet the democratic criteria for membership, but nostalgic pride as wells Russia's traditional penchant for secrecy stand in the way. The notion that its admission is now contingent of the votes of such former Russian dominions as the Baltic states is also too galling for the current Russian political elite to swallow, while the generals would find it hard to stomach the requirement to let NATO comptrollers examine their defense budgets and NATO experts check their weapons. Yet in the longer run, Russia may come to realize that NATO membership will give it greater territorial security, especially in its depopulating far east.*

The belief that globalization is only an extension of American global political dominance was heaven sent for the Russian elite, an occasion to make accusations against America without coming right out and saying so. Brzezinski felt that this was also a way of unifying the disoriented and demoralized post-communist, anti-communist, quasi-communist, nationalistic, and chauvinistic segments of the Russian elite. It also helped Russia identify with the broader anti-globalist sentiment around the world. The Kremlin could once again aspire to a role in the avant-garde of world progress.

The revisionist nationalism of Russia endangered not only democratic reforms on the eastern edges of Europe, but also the integrity of the Atlantic Alliance. The conflict in Georgia showed how important it was for Europe to be decisive and united, especially in combination with American support. After Washington's silence in the face of the massacre in Chechnya, it was not necessary to close one's eyes to brutal imperialism in the name of consistency.

Brzezinski believes that it would be a cardinal error to doom Ukraine in advance to existing in Moscow's shadow. He does not like what he regards as the excessive caution by the European community—frustrated by the mess in Ukraine—in moving ahead with Union membership for the country, and he is pained by the fact that Ukraine is worn out by corruption, poverty, and a sense of having no future. Democratic progress has withered. He feels that if Ukraine turns westward—toward both the EU and NATO—the winners will be not only Ukraine itself, but also Europe and Russia.

Brzezinski is devilishly hardworking, knows what he is looking for, and is sensitive to Russian transgressions. In this case, he hardly needs the skills of a private detective. Recently, the organ of the Russian ministry of foreign affairs published a series of articles intended to show that the Ukrainians are not a genuine nation, but only an offshoot of the Russian people. So why do they want independence?

And what does the longer perspective hold?

> *I expect someday that the Russian president—maybe the one after Medvedev, if Medvedev lasts that long and Putin doesn't come back—may even be a graduate of the Harvard Business School or the London School of Economics. That's not a fanciful speculation; increasingly, the Russian elite tries to send its children to British and American universities, not to Tokyo or Beijing. And at some point, from the Russian point of view, a "Europe" that stretches from Lisbon to Vladivostok will be a welcome vision, because it enables them to keep control of what they treasure, which is the Far East territories.*

Several days after the announcement that Medvedev would pass the baton to Putin, I ask Brzezinski if reshuffling the cards is a blow to Russia's chances for modernization. "No," Zbig says. "But it is an embarrassment, an admission of disdain for public opinion. See—one guy and his assistant have come to the conclusion that it's time for a change, and they simply announce what that change will be."

Brzezinski has been a militant anti-communist his whole life long. Nobody better fits the definition of "hawk." But is he a Russophobe?

> *There's no doubt that there is a depth—an intensity—to human relationships in Russian society that is very heartwarming. And there is a sense of communion that is easy to fit oneself into when you're dealing with Russians who are not part of the KGB or the organizers of the gulag, but Russians who are themselves victims of an oppressive system and whose sense of resentment and deprivation nourishes their souls and makes them more genuine human beings. . . . It's why I like Russians. I like to be among Russians. You may be surprised to hear that I fit in very well, and most of them are very warm towards me, because I often dislike the same things they dislike in their own country.*

# Notes

Brzezinski on the Reagan myth: Zbigniew Brzezinski, *Second Chance: Three Presidents and the Crisis of American Superpower* (New York: Basic Books, 2008), 17.

"Almost in a deterministic Marxist fashion": Zbigniew Brzezinski, *The Choice: Global Domination or Global Leadership* (New York: Basic Books, 2005), 146.

On Putin—"What do we know of him": Zbigniew Brzezinski and Brent Scowcroft, *America and the World. Conversations on the Future of American Foreign Policy.* Moderated by David Ignatius (New York: Basic Books, 2009), 166.

"The person he admired the most": Brzezinski and Scowcroft, *America and the World*, 166.

"Given the rise of China . . .": Brzezinski, *The Choice*, 101.

"I expect someday that the Russian president . . . ": Brzezinski and Scowcroft, *America and the World*, 166.

Personal liking for Russians: Brzezinski and Scowcroft, *America and the World*, 196.

# SECOND CHANCE

**At 3:00 a.m., on November 9, 1979, Brzezinski was awakened by his military assistant, William Odom, who told him that some 250 Soviet missiles had been launched against the United States. Knowing that the President's decision time to order retaliation was three to seven minutes he told Odom to confirm Soviet launch and to make sure that the Strategic Air Command was launching its planes. When Odom called back, he reported that the Soviets had launched an all-out attack, and that 2,200 missiles were heading toward America. Brzezinski was about to call the President when it turned out that the warning was a false alarm.**

"I'm no hero, but this time I stayed calm. I knew that if it were true, then within about half an hour I, and my loved ones, and Washington, and the majority of America would cease to exist. I wanted to be sure that we'd have company," Zbig recalled over a table at a Greek restaurant in July 2011.

Such were the realities of the Cold War.

"You'll miss us yet," said Georgi Arbatov, the adviser to Soviet leaders and America expert, when the USSR collapsed. Brzezinski has never for a minute missed either the Soviet Union or the Soviet divisions stationed around the world. He is uneasy, however, over the wave of self-satisfaction and the feeling hanging in the air that

America can lean back in its armchair and revel in its new imperial status.

Communism of the Chinese variety has not passed away into history. Brzezinski highlighted its roots, the fusion of communism with nationalism, and the influence that a profound feeling of resentment toward both the hated foreigners and its own decadent rulers had on the attractiveness of Chinese communism. "To be sure, the Chinese Communists were never truly a proletarian party. Rather, most of its political leadership was composed of initially disaffected student radicals who became Marxist revolutionaries," he wrote in *The Grand Failure*. Long before membership in the World Trade Organization gave China access to capital and markets, Zbig wrote that "in the course of the next several decades, a more modern and more powerful China will likely become a major political and economic player on the world scene. In the process of guiding that historical rebirth of China, the country's Communist rulers are themselves experiencing a significant redefinition of their guiding ethos. Their dominant outlook, and even their political vocabulary, are becoming less characteristic of the proletariat and more that of a modernizing party of the dictatorship of China's emerging state-sponsored commercial class."

On September 11, 2001, Brzezinski was having dinner in a Beijing hotel with former German Chancellor Helmut Kohl when they heard about the attack on America. It took him a week to get home. Then he was shocked by the extreme arrogance that, in his opinion, was pushing the country into a spiral of self-destruction.

On September 25, 2001, just two weeks after 9/11, in a *Wall Street Journal* op-ed titled "A Plan for Political Warfare," Brzezinski began with two points:

> *Terrorism is political warfare. By deliberately and indiscriminately killing innocents, it is designed to break the will of the opponent. Counterterrorism also has to involve political warfare. It must strive to isolate the terrorists politically in order to extirpate them physically.*
>
> *Not religion as such, but political resentments, often energized by fanatical religious beliefs, fuel terrorism. The current struggle is not against "Islamic terrorism" just as the struggle against the IRA is not against "Christian terrorism." The suppression of terrorist organizations and activities must therefore also address some, if not all, of the political resentments that galvanize support for terrorism.*

How should America respond?

The first US move should be military action. Longer term, it must work to create an international coalition against terror.

"Presumably, some of the early strikes will be aimed at the Taliban regime. Here, the key point is to pursue such operations without becoming involved in a ground campaign."

On October 7, 2001, the United States, Great Britain, Australia, and the Afghan United Front (Northern Alliance) launched Operation Enduring Freedom.

At the end of October 2001, Brzezinski sent a fax to Defense Secretary Donald Rumsfeld. Ten years later, he showed me that fax. It boiled down to this: I know from my own experience that uninvited advice from bystanders is rarely welcome, so I hesitated over whether or not to write. However, I have come to the conclusion that I should share my thoughts with you. I am increasingly concerned that we are becoming excessively involved in the internal politics of Afghanistan. In my opinion our aim should be narrowly and precisely defined: destroying Al-Qaeda's operations in Afghanistan, including the physical liquidation of its leaders. If the Taliban regime interferes we should shove them aside to the degree that we are able to act, but we should not get mixed up in a campaign that has the goal of creating some kind of alternative government. If we achieve our principal aim, then the new government will have to consider whether it is worth harboring Al-Qaeda and taking the risk that we will return to do what is necessary.

The administration remained completely deaf to this advice, and did exactly the opposite.

Nearly a year after the start of America's war on terrorism, "instead of leading a democratic coalition, the United States faces the risk of dangerous isolation," wrote Brzezinski in the *New York Times*. "The Bush administration's definition of the challenge that America confronts has been cast largely in semi-religious terms. The public has been told repeatedly that terrorism is 'evil,' which it undoubtedly is, and that 'evildoers' are responsible for it, which doubtless they are. But beyond these justifiable condemnations, there is a historical void. It is as if terrorism is suspended in outer space as an abstract phenomenon, with ruthless terrorists acting under Satanic inspiration unrelated to any specific motivation."

At the moment when America was sinking waist-deep in Iraq, Brzezinski wrote what the *New York Times* called "the single most lucid and systematic statement of America's twenty-first century security challenges yet to appear." He finished work on *The Choice: Global Domination or Global Leadership* in mid-2003.

Despite all of America's weaknesses, Zbig wrote, the truth was that the country did not have an equal, and would not have one for a long time. Europe was incapable of speaking with a single voice. Neither Japan nor Russia could dream in the long term of dominant power status, if for no other reason than demography. For all its astonishing dynamism, China would remain a poor country for at least two generations. In this situation, America held a special place on the political and economic map of the world. The question was: Would it choose the path of global domination or global leadership?

"Since the end of the Cold War, the European criticism of America as a global bull in the international china shop has become more pervasive and elaborate. The disappearance of the Soviet threat has made such criticism rather risk-free," noted Brzezinski.

He wrote that the unceasing criticism of America for its real and imagined sins was seldom accompanied by reflection on a different scenario—one which could not be ruled out a priori—the scenario of American self-isolation, turning its back on the world. What would happen if Congress, smothering under a burden of debt, forced an administration to pull American troops out of Europe, the Far East, and the Persian Gulf? Some in Europe would chip in to build an army, while others would seek special deals with Moscow. The likelihood of war in Korea and the militarization of Japan would soar in Europe. Iran would dominate the Persian Gulf, creating a threat to adjacent Arab countries.

> *Criticism of America's unilateralism and indifference to European concerns predates the Iraqi issue. . . . Critical views of America did not stem entirely from greater global sensitivity in contrast to selfish American arrogance, as the Europeans were occasionally inclined to suggest. Given Europe's military weakness and political disunity, the condemnations of America provided the Europeans with much-needed compensation for the asymmetry of power between the two sides of the Atlantic. By placing America on the moral and legal defensive, the Europeans created a somewhat more level playing field while arming themselves with reassuring self-righteousness. . . . Europeans would be well advised to weigh prudently the consequences for themselves as well as for others, of a pliant America that subordinates its leadership to the lowest common denominator of collective consensus.*

Brzezinski reminded Americans that hatred and prejudice are stronger emotions than empathy or solidarity. He found similarities between the rhetoric of President George W. Bush and that of Lenin: "Whoever is not with us is against us." He was uneasy at how, in the atmosphere of the "War on Terror," America risked distorting the delicate balance between individual freedom and national security.

Almost four years had passed, Americans once again put their trust in Bush, and Brzezinski spoke out again.

Testifying before the Senate Foreign Relations Committee on February 1, 2007, he didn't mince words. "It is time for the White House to come to terms with two central realities: The war in Iraq is historic, strategic, and mortal calamity. Undertaken under false assumptions, it is undermining America's global legitimacy. Its collateral civilian casualties as well as some abuses are tarnishing America's moral credentials. Only a political strategy that is historically relevant rather than reminiscent of colonial tutelage can provide the needed framework for a tolerable resolution of both the war in Iraq and the intensifying regional tensions."

Brzezinski poured his reflections on what had happened and what could happen if the United States did not make a radical shift in its relations with the world into his next book, *Second Chance: Three Presidents and the Crisis of American Superpower*. It contained not a trace of intellectual triumphalism.

When the Berlin Wall crumbled, Brzezinski publicly asked whether the failure of communism automatically meant the victory of democracy. This also implied the question of whether America was capable of leading the world at a moment when humanity's political and social expectations were being articulated more loudly than in the past, and different cultures and religions were encountering each other daily. Three successive presidents of the United States had the opportunity to fact this question not as a philosophical abstraction but within the dimension of real political choices. None of them came out looking particularly well.

The tempo of Soviet disintegration did not shock George H. W. Bush; and his staff could not understand the forces tearing Yugoslavia apart. American indifference and European impotence led to a bloody outcome in the Balkan crisis. Little was done to politically stabilize or economically rebuild Afghanistan, devastated by a long war, and this caught up with America many years later, and continues to make an impact today.

> *He let his major success—expelling Saddam Hussein from Kuwait in 1991 with impressive military effectiveness and backed by a skillfully contrived political coalition that included Arab states—become strategically inconclusive. This victory should have been exploited to achieve a breakthrough in the Middle Eastern stalemate. . . . It would not have been easy for either side [Israelis and Palestinians] to defy an American leadership that enjoyed unprecedented prestige following the collapse of the Soviet Union and the defeat of Iraq. America was admired and, most importantly, seen as endowed with historical legitimacy. Bush had more leverage to accomplish a breakthrough to peace than any US president since Eisenhower.*

In Brzezinski's opinion, this adroit diplomat and effective soldier squandered the chance that history gave him. His mistakes would come back to haunt America.

Brzezinski described Bill Clinton's presidency as "the Impotence of Good Intentions (and the Price of Self-Indulgence)." His youth, intelligence, and eloquence, as well as his articulate idealism, made him the perfect symbol of a benign but all-powerful America, the world's accepted leader. Unlike his predecessor, Clinton had a global vision. Initially less interested in world affairs, he "replaced the new world order with the concept of 'irreversible globalization.' " (In one of his earlier books Zbig warned that "in both its political rhetoric and its national policymaking, the United States should treat globalization less as a gospel and more as an opportunity for the betterment of the human condition.")

Brzezinski regarded the expansion of NATO and the European Union as the most important achievements of the Clinton presidency. He also placed the NATO intervention in the Balkans, when the Europeans were incapable and the Russians opposed, in the plus column. As Clinton's greatest foreign policy failure he pointed to the failure to resolve the Israel-Palestine conflict despite the agreement in Oslo, the Rabin-Arafat handshake on the White House lawn, and the normalization of Israel-Jordan relations. Clinton himself became an object of admiration, more outside America's borders than at home. Nevertheless, on no occasion did he make the effort to articulate America's role in a tempestuous world. At the end of his second term, America enjoyed the respect of most of the world's countries and correct relations with its allies, but noble intentions could not offset the lack of clear, consistent strategy.

What came next, Brzezinski referred to as a catastrophe. George H. W. Bush's tactical realism was gone. So was Bill Clinton's optimism. What replaced them was a cocktail of ignorance and arrogance, a dogmatic bipolar division of the world into good and evil, and faith in military victory over evil.

"It will take years of deliberate effort and genuine skill to restore America's political credibility and legitimacy," wrote Brzezinski. "Will America have a second chance? Certainly. In large measure that is so because no other power is capable of playing the role America *potentially* can and should play."

America's future acceptability as world leader, wrote Brzezinski, depends on answers to large and complex questions:

*1. Is the American system structurally equipped to formulate and sustain a global policy that not only protects American interests but also promotes global security and well-being?*

*2. Is American society ready to sustain a global leadership role that calls for some degree of responsible self-restraint derived from a basic understanding of global trends?*

*3. Does the nation intuitively sense what the global political awakening implies for America's own future?*

Five years before the Arab Spring, Brzezinski spoke about an explosion of political activism in the societies of many developing countries. Access to television and the Internet amplify feelings of injustice, resentment, antipathy, and envy; this, in turn, challenges both existing national organisms and the global order frequently identified with America. In order to prevent this political awakening from turning against it, America should identify itself more decisively than in the past with ideas of universal human dignity and justice. This also implies respect for a mosaic of cultures and religions. This is one more reason, he reiterated, that impatient democratization, imposed from outside, is doomed to failure.

*On the onset of the global era, a dominant power has therefore no choice but to pursue a foreign policy that is truly globalist in spirit, content, and shape. Nothing could be worse for America, and eventually the world, than if American policy were universally viewed as arrogantly imperial in post-imperial age, mired in a colonial relapse in a postcolonial time, selfishly indifferent in the face of unprecedented global interdependence, and culturally self-righteous in a religiously diverse world. The crisis of American superpower would then become terminal. It is essential—Brzezinski ended his book—that America's second chance after 2008 be more successful than the first for there will be no third chance.*

This is why Brzezinski did not conceal his joy when the Americans elected Obama in November 2008.

In an interview with the German magazine *Stern*, a couple of days after the 2008 presidential election, Brzezinski said: "We might witness the birth of a 21st century America. In fact, this election could define America as the prototype of an eventual global society."

Asked "And why should this be America?" he responded:

> *I cannot imagine another country, neither in Europe, neither in Asia, which could have elected someone as uniquely different as Barack Obama is. Barack Hussein Obama is accepted and cherished, really cherished, because he epitomizes the unique diversity of American society and shares the dominant values of that society.*
> *Which are?*
> *Racial equality, a basic commitment to democracy, a notion of elementary social justice. The notion that some people should not be allowed to be as poor as they are— and that some are not entitled to be quite as rich as they think they can be.*
> *Don't you expect a little too much from a relatively inexperienced Senator from Illinois?*
> *I met him last year, and he made the best impression on me of anyone since John F. Kennedy. He is better equipped in intellect and temperament for the highest office than anyone I can think of in recent memory. He is very different from most American politicians.*
> *What makes him so unique?*
> *A kind of intellectual self-confidence, which reflects real intelligence, not arrogance. A friendliness—but with a distance and a dignity. A little patrician, almost. And a calculating rationality. He does not wave the do-gooders flag. He is*

*an idealist, but not an ideologue. He knows that compromises will be needed.*

*Will Obama be the President of a superpower in decline?*

*No. That's nonsense and often said with a lot of schadenfreude. The matter of fact is, that the era of American superpower stupidity is over, the time of self-isolation. Under President Bush, we acted arrogant, unilateralist—worst of all—driven by fear. A culture of fear was cultivated by this administration, which replaced the Statue of Liberty as a symbol for America with Guantánamo. America has lost its confidence. This is one of the worst legacies of the Bush era. But that will come to an end now, very quickly. . . .*

*Will Obama expect more engagement from Europe, Germany?*

*The American people expect this. If the Europeans want to give us only nice advice, but expect us to do the heavy lifting—then don't expect America necessarily to listen to these advises. Europeans will no longer have the alibi of Bush's bad policy. But let's be clear: there are no alibis for us anymore, either. We will have to consult, share decisions and cooperate.*

Before Barack Obama moved to the White House, Brzezinski wrote in a *New York Times* piece that "though US leadership has been essential to global stability and development, the cumulative effects of national self-indulgence, financial irresponsibility, an unnecessary war and ethical transgressions have discredited that leadership. Making matters worse is the global economic crisis." He concluded on what he called a parochial note: "Unfortunately, the American public is woefully undereducated about the wider world. Barack Obama will have to strive to make Americans understand the novel dimensions of global realities. Without sounding overly partisan, I believe that he has unique intellectual and rhetorical gifts for doing just that."

When Obama received the Nobel Peace Prize, Brzezinski felt that he deserved it for his strategic vision, new language, openness, readiness for redefinition, and new articulation of the aims and role of the United States in the world. In an article titled "From Hope to Audacity," in *Foreign Affairs* (January–February 2010), he wrote that "three urgent issues—the Israeli-Palestinian conflict, Iran's nuclear ambitions, and the Afghan-Pakistani challenge—will test Barack Obama's ability to meaningfully change US policy, acknowledging that his foreign policy had generated more expectations than strategic breakthroughs." Three urgent issues—the Israeli-Palestinian conflict, Iran's nuclear ambitions, and the Afghan-Pakistani challenge—will test Barack Obama's ability to meaningfully change US policy, acknowledging that his foreign policy had generated more expectations than strategic breakthroughs."

This was in part because the president must treat foreign policy as something of a part-time job. The economic crisis and reform of the health-care system take up much of his time. In this situation, much depends on his advisors and the government apparatus, who prefer caution and continuity over new approaches and action.

At the very beginning of his acquaintance with Obama, Zbig told me that he would willingly offer his advice, but a role as official adviser would not be beneficial to either of them. He has good relations with the president. These days, they meet in larger groups, not face to face—usually when the White House invites former national security advisers for consultations with the president. Obama has not been stinting with elegant gestures directed at Zbig. For instance, Brzezinski flew in a presidential aircraft as head of the American delegation on the 25th anniversary of the Chernobyl tragedy. The US ambassador greeted him at the airport at six o'clock in the morning. There may indeed have been no honor guard, but this was Ukraine, not China.

— ★ —

# Notes

"Semi-religious" nature of Bush vision: Brzezinski, "Confronting Anti-American Grievances," *The New York Times*, September 1, 2002.

Brzezinski's post-electoral assessment of Obama: "The Global Political Awakening," *The New York Times*, December 16, 2008.

# THE NEW CHESSBOARD

Napoleon, the German shepherd, offers me a friendly reception in front of the Brzezinski home in MacLean, Virginia, which is more modest than I imagined but nevertheless has a tennis court and stands on a five-acre lot. A moment later, my host opens the front door. He is wearing a black tracksuit with the logo of *Morning Joe*, the popular MSNBC show co-hosted by his daughter Mika. Zbig is in good shape, with no hint of a belly on his 5'9" frame, whether this results from his genes, his diet, or tennis. He plays three times a week, weather permitting, and once a week in the winter—always singles. I recall how Robert Gates remembered Zbig from the Carter White House, "He debated like he played tennis—to win and to win all the time." He is relaxed, not at all the way he comes across on TV when he fixes his interlocutor with his gaze and seems to be waiting for a slip-up. The wrinkles lining his face belie his age momentarily, but his silhouette and movements tell a different story.

I kiss his wife's hand—a Polish custom that is dying out, but only slowly. Emilie Brzezinski, née Benes, is a relative of Edward Benes, the one-time president of Czechoslovakia. She sculpts in wood, using enormous segments of tree trunks ten feet tall. At the end of the visit, she leads me around the gigantic sheds that serve her as a studio and proudly shows off the collection of electric chainsaws she uses to supplement her chisel. Before that, she served tea with delectable homemade cake and then went off to work. Her husband praises the vegetables she raises in the garden.

Until recently, she kept bees and rabbits. Near the small table where we sit are my host's family heirlooms: the helmet his brother wore when he fought in Normandy and was seriously wounded in Holland and the cap that his father Tadeusz Brzezinski, a prewar Polish diplomat, wore as a lieutenant in the victorious 1920 battle against the Bolsheviks outside Warsaw. "And here is something more optimistic," says Zbig, "the saber that I received from the government of the Republic of Poland for my contribution to the accession of Poland to NATO." He fetches a pair of elegant old crystal glasses and a bottle of Drambuie. I use the fact that I am driving as an excuse, but the truth is that I want to be at my most alert. There will be no joking around here. The professor operates to a demanding standard.

I ask him whether he will leave his grandchildren a better world than the one in which he began his political career. He responds:

> *It's too early to tell because I'm in no hurry to make my exit. I do not believe that we are facing the inevitable collapse of America and the downfall of the West, or global anarchy. The fact that we recognize the possibility of such a scenario and are beginning to understand what it would mean is a source of moderate optimism for me. The world I grew up in was much worse than the present. There is no Hitler or Stalin, and I cannot see the possibility of a repetition of them in any form, unless everything were to collapse and everyone had to fight for survival.*

He has written many times that the world needs leadership and that no one can replace America in that role, yet in the meantime the leader is in poor condition. The leader is losing wars and cannot put its own house in order. The muscles are atrophying, the image is fading, and respect is crumbling. So I ask Brzezinski if the world still needs America. And he tells me: "If America fell into a deep and malignant crisis that paralyzed it for a long time and prevented it from acting on the international scene, the consequences for everyone would be extremely adverse. Most intelligent statesmen realize this. This is true both of those who have a stake in the status quo—the Europeans—and those who perceive themselves as the beneficiaries of the changes that are underway—the Chinese. They all know that America, regardless of its mistakes, is in the final analysis the ultimate source of global stability."

Does this mean that, all the schadenfreude aside, the majority of the world roots for America?

"It roots in a quiet way," Zbig replies. "A Chinese statesman recently told me, 'Please don't let America decline too quickly.' Today there is still no alternative to America. There is still no alternative to the dollar. And there is no one who, as America does, could guarantee the security of many countries in so many parts of the world."

I try to draw him into macroeconomics: Paradoxically, the triumph of the West in the ideological rivalry and the victory of the market in the rivalry with the planned economy has not strengthened the position of the West, but instead hastened its erosion. Capital has been emboldened to flow where it can earn more, and it does not look as if that stream can be restrained.

Zbig replies without a moment's consideration:

> *Since it cannot be restrained, then protectionism would be ineffective. On the other hand, a different scenario is possible, and even highly likely.*
>
> *The social tensions that accompany and will continue to accompany changes in world relations will at some point force us to seek a new grand compromise. There will be a need for more regulation because the scale of deregulation has led to an explosion of economically ineffective and purely financial speculation with extraordinary and morally unacceptable profits for*

*a handful, and pauperization for the many. This cannot go on without end. Although the appeal to class conflict is not a very attractive idea in American conditions, in view of the situation the revelation of the glaring and evidently unjust disparity of outcomes and fortunes might speak to people. . . . I do not accept the idea that we live in times where the future is predetermined, that technology decides everything and that we have completely lost control of it. We can get it back. The moment of sobriety will come. There is a need for more regulation and better standardization of regulation on an international scale, so that no large region feels that submitting to regulations places it in an unfavorable situation in relation to its rivals.*

*America is facing at least several very difficult and to a large degree lost years. The European Union will not fall apart. Even though it is torn by internal troubles, its leaders have begun to realize how high the stakes are, and also that the construction is faulty and that there is a need to cast off the burdens that are crushing it. But if we do not find a cure for the violent economic withering of the traditional powers, then the global consequences will be very grim.*

I ask whether the former ideological rivals of the West, Russia and China, will behave rationally.

"I think so," he replies. "In 2007, when America began stumbling badly in economic turns, Russia reacted with overt schadenfreude, smirking at America and enjoying America's problems. But that changed very quickly—by 2008, the Russians were panicking. They were painfully aware that they do not live in some separate space, that the interdependencies are stronger than they had thought. I do not believe that they are smirking today and feeling triumphant because of America's troubles."

I ask whether the shuffling of posts in the Kremlin is a blow to this chance for modernization. And he responds:

*No, but on the other hand it is embarrassing, an expression of a disregard for public opinion. Not even for a moment was there any attempt to dress it up in the robes of procedure. One guy and his assistant came to the conclusion that it was time for a change, and that they could simply announce that change. For many Russians, Putin is the guarantor of stability, and that means a lot to them. Perhaps Putin may appeal in the short term to Russian nationalism, but that's a cul-de-sac. Russia has stopped being a closed country. Many people, especially the young, travel around the world. They look, they study, and they fear ostracism. In the coming decade, there may be a consolidation of centralized power and a regression in the tempo of modernization, but it will quickly become clear once again that this is not the way. It will lead to more internal pressure to become a part of something bigger than Russia, to become a part of Europe, a Europe with strong links to America. Russia still means enormous nepotism and corruption, but this is openly spoken and written about. The atmosphere has changed. People are learning about their own history. This knowledge adds up. In the future, the only sensible scenario for Russia is gravitation toward the West. Motivation for this will undoubtedly come from the situation on its own underbelly, as well as from demography.*

*China is a different matter. It has capacity to do a lot of damage if it begins acting irrationally, especially if nationalistic tendencies gain the upper hand. But for the time being, the Chinese elite is behaving responsibly and rationally.*

I remark that China is deliberately downplaying its global aspirations, but at the same time it is building aircraft carriers and taking economic control of Africa, and I ask whether this is a symptom of imperial ambitions.

He leads me over to a globe, points his finger at China, and says, "China is strategically encircled by powers that are either unfriendly or that stand in its way—the American fleet, the Russian fleet, and finally India with its much more favorable access to the sea. India is also building aircraft carriers. The Chinese aircraft carrier is directed more against India than toward conquering the world. It is a weapon that China can resort to in the event of a serious conflict with India, or if India should close the Indian Ocean to Chinese ships."

Those ships, I add, that are swamping the world with cheap merchandise produced by people whose basic rights are often suppressed. How to defend human rights, which China does not respect, while at the same time maintaining good relations with China? He answers: "Do both one and the other. Develop mutual relations, if they are advantageous, without forgetting about human rights, and give them to understand that relations would be even more advantageous if China took more account of human rights. But say this tactfully, without acting superior, and without forgetting about one's own sins in this regard, especially in the case of America."

Does Europe have stronger moral foundations to stand on in a human rights campaign aimed at China?

Brzezinski has his doubts about this for several reasons: "In the first place, the European powers have not covered themselves in glory in modern Chinese history—in China, in the times of Queen Victoria's reign, the British Empire was probably the greatest institution for drug trafficking in history. Second, the Chinese know perfectly well that Europeans are inconsistent, and that there are in fact no Europeans—there are Britons, the French, Germans, and sometimes Poles."

I ask if he senses nostalgia for Mao in China.

"In certain party circles, yes. But it is nostalgia at a distance, somewhat abstract," he answers. "If a party dignitary reminisces tenderly about Mao, he has the certainty that the Chairman will not be coming back to send him off to the countryside for rehabilitation for some trivial reason. This resembles to a degree the great admiration for Peter the Great, who was cruel, not to mention Stalin, on the part of some Russians."

Is China an ever-more-modern express train rushing with tremendous speed into the future, or an express bound for disaster any moment now? He responds:

> *Disaster cannot be excluded, but the characteristics of the Chinese include caution and patience. The express is slowing down on its own. I expect China to undergo a series of grave social shocks. They think this themselves and speak openly about it. However, I do not feel that this will lead to any sudden, dramatic break or the fall of the system. China today is more stable than India, which boasts about being the world's largest democracy but where more than 50 percent of the women are illiterate, where we have unprecedented income inequality, gigantic corruption, and slower social progress than in China. Indian democracy is comparable, at best, with Britain in the mid-nineteenth century. When we remember that the internet and television carry images of iniquity, it is worth considering the stability of India when speculating about the stability of China.*

From there, it is a short step to Afghanistan and Pakistan.

> *The situation in that region should become an area of cooperation by many actors—mainly the neighboring countries. America should either bring this about or pack up and go home. The latter option must be accompanied by the awareness that it would result in a tragedy for the Afghans, the destabilization of Pakistan, the probable escalation of ten-*

*sions with India, and the spilling over of extremism into the adjacent post-Soviet countries—Turkmenistan, Tajikistan, and Uzbekistan—and this would affect the Russians and potentially even Iran and China. Then the region would be in danger of a generalized Balkan war. That is why I have used the term "greater Balkans" for this region. This very scenario, which is far from imaginary, places a very powerful lever in the hands of the United States. Washington should remind the countries of the region about this: If you do not quickly join in a serious search for a stable solution, you will pay a high price. And America itself? Terrorist groups can hit us today, regardless of whether we are present in Afghanistan or Pakistan or not.*

Zbig's recipe for Iran?

*Calm and patience. There are indications that Iran is coming to resemble Turkey. The educational level, the access to universities, the participation of women in public life—all of this could come as a surprise in a country ruled by theocrats. A few years after Ataturk's experiments, a similar process got under way in Iran. In the cities, the country is ready for the next stage of modernization, but external pressure on Tehran builds up the alliance of theocracy and nationalism. If we remain patient and offer security guarantees to the neighboring countries in case Iran becomes a nuclear country, the present ruling structure will trip up and Iran will follow a path similar to Turkey.*

Zbig speaks about Turkey on various occasions. Receiving the Prix Tocqueville from former French president Valéry Giscard d'Estaing in Normandy in September 2011, he extended the term *Atlantic community* to embrace in the long term not only Russia, but also Turkey. "In the first place, Turkey is proof that both democratization and modernization can be reconciled with Islam. Secondly, the peaceful cooperation of Turkey with its Middle Eastern neighbors serves the security of the West in that region. Thirdly, an increasingly secular and pro-Western Turkey can dilute the attractions of Islamic extremism and foster stabilization in Central Asia, which is also in the interest of Europe and Russia. Additionally, a democratic Turkey can serve as an inducement to the Arab countries in their march toward stable democracy."

I allude to *The Grand Chessboard*, the book that Brzezinski published in 1997, the same year that President Bill Clinton said in his second inaugural address that "at the dawn of the 21st century America stands alone as the world's indispensable nation." I ask him whether he would risk a description of that chessboard over the coming quarter century.

"After the fall of the Soviet Union," he says, "only a single queen remained on the world chessboard—America. We are entering a period in which several equivalents of the queen are appearing. One queen may manage to maintain a greater margin for maneuver—that will still be America—but two or three other queens could appear. That will make for a far more complicated game. But it is not a game in which I foresee any kind of hegemony, any single new queen."

We say our farewells. Several months later, many of Brzezinski's thoughts from our interview can be found in his new book, *Strategic Vision: America and the Crisis of Global Power*.

The domination of the West is entering its twilight. The European Union is behaving as if it had set as its goal creating the most luxurious old-age home in the world—this is Zbig's definition. Although China with its backward civilization and authoritarian political system offers no alluring alternative to America as a model of a modern, democratic, affluent country, it can become America's main rival in the battle for political influence. Even today, it represents an attractive model for countries mired in poverty, for which the choice between democracy and authoritarianism has secondary importance.

Brzezinski is far from writing America off. He counts off its enormous advantages: economic strength despite persistent inequalities; a capacity for innovation that results in part from the enterprise culture and in part from the potential of its higher education; a relatively strong demographic base, especially in comparison with Europe, Japan, and Russia, which results in no small measure from its ability to attract and assimilate immigrants; an aptitude for mobilizing itself and, in favorable circumstances, undertaking the work of renewal; a resource-rich base for a society free of separatist tensions and threats from its neighbors; and finally an integral system of values and a deeply rooted tradition of democracy.

The world after America: By 2025, not Chinese but chaotic. And afterward?

America is still not Rome, and China is not yet Byzantium. There is much that America can still do. It can help the West pull itself up out of its apathy by proposing a rejuvenating cure, while at the same time playing the role of trusted adviser to the world of Asia, which is dynamic but full of conflicts that are already visible as they gather on the horizon. The conclusion: "America must adopt a dual role. It must be the promoter and guarantor of greater and broader unity in the West, and it must be the balancer and conciliator between the major powers in the East."

Yet before America can play any of these roles, it must first pull itself together. It is facing challenges of which a decisive majority of the population is simply unaware, and which the majority of the politicians avoid like the plague. Zbig has long been irritated and worried by the ignorance of Americans when it comes to the outside world. He mentions this in one breath among America's cardinal sins and liabilities, along with mounting debt, a flawed financial system, widening income inequality, decaying infrastructure, and, related to public ignorance, America's increasingly gridlocked and highly partisan political system.

Although he is fascinated with Asia, Zbig devotes a great deal of space to Europe and the definition of its eastern borderlands. This will, in turn, define the eastern border of the West. Will it encompass Turkey and Russia? His vision of the young Europeans who, resembling the American pioneers before them, will be attracted to Siberia and Anatolia, has an air of utopia to it, but nevertheless it all seems more realistic than the vision of crowds greeting our tanks in Baghdad with flowers. And wasn't the sudden downfall of the Soviet superpower, armed to the teeth, itself a kind of utopian dream?

The amount of optimism remaining in him is astonishing. Perhaps this is the echo of that existential battle against communism that was won far earlier than could have been anticipated.

Can Zbig count on a fair judgment by history? I doubt it. Contemporaries are rarely objective, but history often fails to correct the myths and prejudices. In American popular opinion, Ronald Reagan is a great president while Jimmy Carter is a failure, one of fate's incomprehensible mistakes.

Today, when politicians continually sniff to see which way the wind is blowing and change their opinions more frequently than their clothes, the steadiness of Reagan's convictions and his faith in the rightness of his actions looks extraordinary. His stubbornness stemmed precisely from the strength of his convictions. Few remember today that he had no idea of what to do about China, the Middle East, or mediocre schools. People remember his optimism and his contagious faith in America and its future. On the other hand, Americans recall Carter mainly for the fiasco of the attempted freeing of the hostages in Tehran, and for high inflation. Yet he was the first president of the United States to publicly and consistently question during the Cold War, the legitimacy of the Soviets' rule in their own country.

"I believe historians and political observers alike have failed to appreciate the importance of Jimmy Carter's contribution to the collapse of the Soviet Union and the end of the Cold War," writes Robert Gates, Director of Central Intelligence under President George H. W. Bush, and Secretary of Defense under the George W. Bush and Barack Obama administrations. "In fact," writes Gates, "Carter prepared the ground for Reagan. He took the first steps to strip away the mask of Soviet ascendancy and exploit the reality of Soviet vulnerability."

A year after the end of the Carter administration, former White House chief of staff Hamilton Jordan wrote that "the notion that Dr. Zbigniew Brzezinski had the President's ear spread to the extent that many thought he had Carter's mind as well." Of course, this was not the case. Carter was a very intelligent, independent-minded man. Neither in Washington, nor in Moscow, nor in Beijing, Tokyo, London, Paris, or Bonn, however, was there any doubt that that Carter's vision and strategy were both to an enormous degree indebted to Brzezinski. He was the one who made his boss aware of the need for a more steadfast course in the face of Moscow's aggressive policy, and pushed him constantly in this direction. He understood perfectly the source of the adversary's weakness and did not hesitate to attack its soft underbelly.

Many years later the dissidents in the communist countries, despite their frequent differences, agree about the enormous role that Carter's human-rights doctrine played in the dismantling of the system. Walter Lippmann, the American commentator who was an informal adviser to many presidents, wrote many years ago that we should all "plant a tree under which we will never sit." Carter and Brzezinski sowed the seeds of human rights in the Soviet bloc, and those seeds sprouted with astonishing rapidity.

# BIBLIOGRAPHY

Albright, Madeleine. *Memo to the President Elect.* New York: HarperCollins, 2008.

Astor, Gerald. *Presidents at War: From Truman to Bush, the Gathering of Military Power to Our Commanders in Chief.* Hoboken, NJ: John Wiley & Sons, Inc., 2006.

Brzezinski, Zbigniew. *The Choice: Global Domination or Global Leadership.* New York: Basic Books, 2005.

———. *The Grand Failure: The Birth and Death of Communism in the Twentieth Century.* New York: Collier Books, 1990.

———. *Ideology and Power in Soviet Politics.* New York: Frederick A. Praeger, 1976.

———. *Power and Principle. Memoirs of the National Security Adviser 1977–1981.* New York: Farrar, Strauss and Giroux, 1983.

———. *Second Chance. Three Presidents and the Crisis of American Superpower.* New York: Basic Books, 2008.

———. *Strategic Vision: America and the Crisis of Global Power.* New York: Basic Books, 2012.

# BIBLIOGRAPHY

Brzezinski, Zbigniew, and Brent Scowcroft. *America and the World: Conversations on the Future of American Foreign Policy.* Moderated by David Ignatius. New York: Basic Books, 2009.

Bundy, William P, ed. *Two Hundred Years of American Foreign Policy.* New York: New York University Press, 1977.

Carter, Jimmy. *Keeping Faith. Memoirs of a President.* New York: Bantam Books, 1982.

———. *White House Diary.* New York: Farrar, Strauss and Giroux, 2010.

———. *Why Not the Best? The First Fifty Years.* Fayetteville, AR: University of Arkansas Press, 1996.

Cooley, John. *Unholy Wars. Afghanistan, America and International Terrorism.* 3rd ed. London and Sterling, VA: Pluto Press, 2002,

Daaler, Ivo H., and I. M. Destler. *In the Shadow of the Oval Office: Profiles of the National Security Advisers and the Presidents They Served—from JFK to George W. Bush.* New York: Simon & Schuster, 2011.

Estulin, Daniel. *The True Story of the Bilderberg Group.* Walterville, OR: Trine Day, 2009.

Friedrich, Carl J., and Zbigniew Brzezinski. *Totalitarian Dictatorship and Autocracy.* Cambridge, MA: Harvard University Press, 1956.

Gates, Robert M. *From the Shadows: The Ultimate Insider's Story of Five Presidents and How They Won the Cold War.* New York: Simon & Schuster, 2007.

Gelb, Leslie H. *Power Rules: How Common Sense Can Rescue American Foreign Policy.* New York: Harper Perennial, 2010.

# BIBLIOGRAPHY

Isaacson, Walter. *Kissinger: A Biography.* New York: Simon & Schuster, 2005.

Jordan, Hamilton. *Crisis: The Last Year of the Carter Presidency.* New York: Putnam Adult, 1982.

MacMillan, Margaret. *Nixon and Mao: The Week That Changed the World.* New York: Random House, 2008.

Mondale, Walter F. *The Good Fight: A Life in Liberal Politics.* New York: Scribner, 2010.

Prados, John. *Keepers of the Keys: A History of National Security from Truman to Bush.* New York: William Morrow and Company, 1991.

Rockefeller, David. *Memoirs.* New York: Random House, 2002.

Roseboom, Eugene Holloway, and Alfred E. Eckes Jr. *A History of Presidential Elections: From George Washington to Jimmy Carter.* 4th edition. New York: Collier Books, 1979.

Ross, Dennis, and David Makovsky. *Myths, Illusions, and Peace Finding a New Direction for America in the Middle East.* New York: Viking Adult, 2009.

Rothkopf, David. *Running the World: The Inside Story of the National Security and the Architects of American Power.* New York: PublicAffairs, 2006.

Sick, Gary. *October Surprise: America's Hostages in Iran and the Election of Ronald Reagan.* New York: Crown, 1991.

Turner, Stansfield. *Burn Before Reading: Presidents, CIA Directors, and Secret Intelligence.* New York: Hyperion, 2005.

Tyler, Patrick. *A World of Trouble: The White House and the Middle East—from the Cold War to the War on Terror.* New York: Farrar, Straus and Giroux, 2010.

# BIBLIOGRAPHY

———. *A Great Wall: Six Presidents and China: An Investigative History.* New York: PublicAffairs, 2000.

Vaughan, Parick. *Zbigniew Brzezinski (Polska wersja jezykowa).* Warsaw, Poland: Świat Książki, 2010.

Weiser, Benjamin. *A Secret Life: The Polish Officer, His Covert Mission, and the Price He Paid to Save His Country.* New York: PublicAffairs, 2005.

Wilford, Hugh. *The Mighty Wurlitzer: How the CIA Played America.* Cambridge, MA: Harvard University Press, 2009.

Woodward, Bob. *Veil: The Secret Wars of the CIA 1981–1987.* New York: Simon & Schuster, 2005.

www.ingramcontent.com/pod-product-compliance
Lightning Source LLC
LaVergne TN
LVHW041540070426
835507LV00011B/844